ALEXANDER THE GREAT

ALEXANDER THE GREAT

Leadership Lessons from the Man Who Created an Empire

LANCE KURKE, PhD

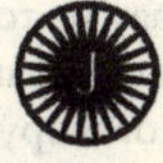

JAICO PUBLISHING HOUSE

Ahmedabad Bangalore Chennai
Delhi Hyderabad Kolkata Mumbai

Published by Jaico Publishing House
A-2 Jash Chambers, 7-A Sir Phirozshah Mehta Road
Fort, Mumbai - 400 001
jaicopub@jaicobooks.com
www.jaicobooks.com

Published in arrangement with
HarperCollins Leadership,
a division of HarperCollins Focus, LLC.

Original English-language edition published as
The Wisdom of Alexander the Great
by AMACOM,
a division of the American Management Association, International,
New York.

ALEXANDER THE GREAT
ISBN 978-81-8495-043-4

First Jaico Impression: 2009
Fourth Jaico Impression (New Cover): 2023

Printed by
Repro India Limited, Mumbai

CONTENTS

FOREWORD

Alexander the Great as a leadership model for the modern world? Dr. Lance Kurke brings to life the heroic exploits of this most extraordinary leader and derives from them clear and concise lessons for those who aspire to be today's effective leaders.

Truly great leaders change the world around them. They instill in their followers a cohesive identity and clear purpose. They treat difficult problems as addressable opportunities. Whether it involves a historical figure or the modern business organization, the leadership process creates sustained meaning, shared interpretation, and joint action in the organization. This is what Dr. Kurke defines as the process of enactment. In his hands, enactment derives from four leadership processes: reframing problems, building alliances, establishing identity, and directing symbols. Taken together, these four processes create new realities. They influence the choice of priorities and partners and create unity through shared understanding of the importance of chosen actions.

Alexander the Great is a superbly readable book that rewards its reader with thought-provoking lessons applicable to current business problems. It is written for the busy executive, manager, or military leader in that it is a collage of short self-contained stories that can be savored in small segments of valuable free time. All the stories are interrelated, and Dr. Kurke ties them into a neat bundle that, considered in its totality, is a complete and coherent process for leadership.

In this book's conclusion, Dr. Kurke suggests that we should all have heroes and read about them—and learn to tell stories. Dr. Kurke has his own hero in Alexander the Great, and he certainly is a wonderful storyteller.

Steven F. Goldstone
Former Chairman and CEO, RJR Nabisco

PREFACE

Leadership cannot be taught, but it can be learned. This book will help you to learn about leadership.

We are all students of leadership, though some of us are much more sentient about our explorations. Because I help people learn about leadership (having worked with many hundreds of CEOs, managing partners, executive directors, presidents, mayors, chairmen and chairwomen, colonels, and superintendents in all kinds of organizations), I have presumed to say something about how exceptional leaders employ their skills.

However, I find it difficult to help these leaders learn to be more effective without a clear, specific, tangible context. In this book, this context is Alexander the Great. I believe that this book, using Alexander as the context, can help you better understand how to be a better leader by surreptitiously observing how a great one acted in history.

While Alexander provides the context, the theory of enactment provides the learning framework for developing leadership. Enactment, like most important lessons that derive from academic explorations, has been slow to find general acceptance. Only now is enactment becoming known outside of the academic community. Leaders who embrace its power will outperform their peers, and perseverance will be strongly rewarded.

It is said that chronology is the last refuge of the feeble-minded and the only resort of the historian. By apology, I am not trained as an historian, but rather in the social sciences of organizational behavior and theory. My interests are strategic planning and executive education (in leadership and strategic planning). Thus, I escape this refuge. This book is not chronological for three reasons. First, almost all the other wonderful works on Alexander are chronological, and we don't need yet another retelling. I am trying to convey a sense of his leadership and strategic genius. Second, I am a storyteller, and this is a story. As a business educator, I want to inform and teach, not just tell history. History is, therefore, my tool, not my constraint. (Having said this, I strive to be as accurate to the historical truth as I understand it.) Third, I have attempted to group the vignettes of Alexander's life into categories that, taken together, support each other. The imposition of the guiding framework is utterly a figment of my obsessive investigation of enactment. (Were I a braver writer, I would have written a fictional account using the rubric of Alexander's diary.) Consequently, the vignettes that make up this man's life are, in my opinion, best grouped by category or lesson. By "best," I mean useful to modern leaders.

In this book I can't promise to make you a great leader. I can't even promise to make you a good leader. But I can promise to make you a *better* leader.

Hindsight is a double-edged sword. Too much of it and the past seems inevitable. With too little hindsight, a panoramic perspective is impossible. Accordingly, I have tried simultaneously to retain the lack of inevitability of the past while gaining the benefit of historical perspective.

Sources: How Do We Know What We Know?

One of the single most important concerns of any leader—military, business, or civilian—is intelligence. Not the IQ kind (I've known some good leaders who are not so bright), but the kind that yields information. What gossip and rumors do we listen to? Why? Whose report is to be believed? When do we trust the reports of Wall Street analysts? Does a particular board informant have an agenda unknown to us? Where did the consultant get her information, and why should we believe her? Do we trust this industry analyst? Is our intelligence about the competition accurate? Is our internal strategic-planning analysis of strengths accurate, or is it overstated for political reasons? Similarly, are our weaknesses understated? You can see (and you know from experience) that knowledge is power. Power, though, derives from *accurate* intelligence, *accurate* information, and *accurate* knowledge. The questions are: How do you know what information is accurate, and what do you believe?

In a parallel vein, how do historians know what they know about Alexander the Great, and why should you believe them? If you can't believe the sources, then are you learning bogus lessons? What knowledge do we believe? Why? When?

Sources: Accounting Irregularities

In historical writing, we compare the various sources of data and make informed judgments, just like any decision maker in any organization.

All of the classical sources exaggerate the losses of Alexander's opponents. Why? Well, each author has a perspective to air. Plutarch, for example, seemed to make his heroes bigger than life (unnecessary in Alexander's case), so he usually reported the higher numbers asserted. Others seem to opt for more accuracy, though the second great battle, at Issus, shows the disparities. Arrian, generally considered the most accurate and reliable historian, reported 100,000 Persians and 10,000 cavalry killed at this battle. This number *must* be greatly inflated. Alexander lost perhaps 1,000 troops, and even a ten-to-one casualty ratio is unheard of, except at Zama, Agincourt, and a few other battles. Surely, Issus did not qualify as such a lopsided battle.

Exaggeration has many friends, and few enemies. CEOs take credit for successes, real or not, and inflated numbers make the victory seem all that much more magnificent. The smaller the loss, the less troubling it is to the board of directors, so exaggeration works for leaders in both directions, if properly managed. So what we look for in strategic planning, accounting auditing, and history are independent audits.

The victor writes history, which is hardly independent. Successful CEOs are generally believed. When they fail, their opponent's version becomes truth. Truth is seldom absolute in battle. Even with modern battlefield intelligence, leaders often remain unclear about events. Histories written by those who saw only a portion of the field, and who necessarily rely on the similarly biased observations of others, necessarily provide inaccurate data. Sometimes modern historians can compare all the reports and do a fair job of sorting out the inconsistencies and prejudices.

Alexander's exploits are documented in four good and extant classical sources: Plutarch, Arrian, Diodorus, and Curtius. All four provide secondhand histories, but with the benefit of the authors' direct access to the original reports. This would be like historians in 2,000 years finding four histories of George Washington (whose authors had access to all original documents or copies), but essentially no original documents, except for carved inscriptions that survived with the four secondhand histories. Each history will have some problems, but if we take them all together, we can construct a pretty accurate picture. That is exactly what historians have done with the four classical sources. As a result, we seem to have a quite accurate picture of Alexander's campaigns.

In business, one could point out that truth, honest reporting, stretching the rules, opinion, fact, and fraud often are not easy to separate. That is why we rely on independent audits, due diligence, and outside consultants. While each is fallible, taken together, like the classics on Alexander, they give a better, more accurate picture.

ACKNOWLEDGMENTS

Books are not the work of one individual. Authors need support, comfort, encouragement, advice, a distant mirror, and a mind that's not too close to the manuscript. I have a lot of people to thank for making this book possible.

I relied on lay readers, rather than professional historians, although Jim McClenahan comes close to that qualification. Jim is a retired Marine colonel with an unmatched eye for detail. He read the entire manuscript twice and found every factual and grammatical error. As a former teacher of military history, his command of Alexander very nearly equaled my own—he kept me honest, though mistakes, of course, remain my responsibility. My longtime friend Dave Ball (a former international CEO who was based in India for years) read and critiqued the manuscript with a critical eye. To an embarrassing extent, he produced this work; I suppose it's similar to how a producer keeps a director on track. Dave practically rewrote the first full draft, and accordingly, my debt to him is great. Thank you, Dave. Finally, my dean, Jim Stalder, a former managing partner at PricewaterhouseCoopers, has a long-term interest in Alexander, and he kindly read an early version of this manuscript, encouraging me to define my purpose and pursue it to publication.

My family has been invaluable. I found my greatest inspiration in my daughter Jamie, who by third grade was a regular publisher of books at school, and who inspired, cajoled, and generally encouraged me to complete this work. My son Max is the king of the household, so I learned a lot about leading from him. Mindi Righter and her husband, Jeff, and my grandson, Neo, stayed in the background, offering encouragement by their presence and patience. Florri Mendelson is a gifted manager and taught me much about leadership, people, and organizations. My brother Matt is a daily influence on my life, and any wise decisions I make are, in part, attributable to his love. Since my mother's death, my sister Sue Heine and her husband, Larry, have been my life's rudder. Much of my success is attributable to them. May my father, John, enjoy this book. May Ben learn from it. Bill would have devoured it.

Friends make everything possible. First and foremost, Michael and Wendy Kumer have stood by me more than any friends should be expected to. They kept me sane while I finished this work. Mark Seabright has been there for me as long as I have been sentient. Firdaus Bagasrawala was encouraging at a critical point. Norna Kissane has been supportive for more than a decade. Meg Brindle helped me to refine my thoughts on enactment, and I owe her a professional thank you. Of my colleagues, Jim Weber has been the most chronically supportive, although many unnamed colleagues of mine at Duquesne, unbeknownst to them, have nurtured me. Clients and business associates too numerous to name influenced my developing thoughts about leadership, some without realizing the importance of their influence, but a few warrant mention: Bob Bozzone, Linda

Dickerson, Andy Field, Steven Goldstone, Bill Lowry, Bill McGuire, John Polutnik, Dave Reece, Larry Shekell, Art Stroyd, Jeff Yannazzo, and Ted Wilke. All of these people made this work possible, and to them all I have incurred a debt of gratitude. Finally, my most important teachers have been my students, both MBA and executive. This book perhaps owes the most to them.

A great leader would have impeccable integrity, be helpful, communicate neither too much nor too little, keep a sense of humor, be motivating, patient, and challenging, yet believe in you. Such is my editor, Christina McLaughlin at AMACOM. Thank you, Christina.

Lance B. Kurke
Pittsburgh, Pennsylvania

Courtesy of Cornell University Library, Making of America Digital Collection. From Benjamin Ide Wheeler, "Alexander the Great: The Invasion of Asia and the Battle of the Granicus, *The Century,* vol. 57, no. 3, Jan. 1899, p. 363.

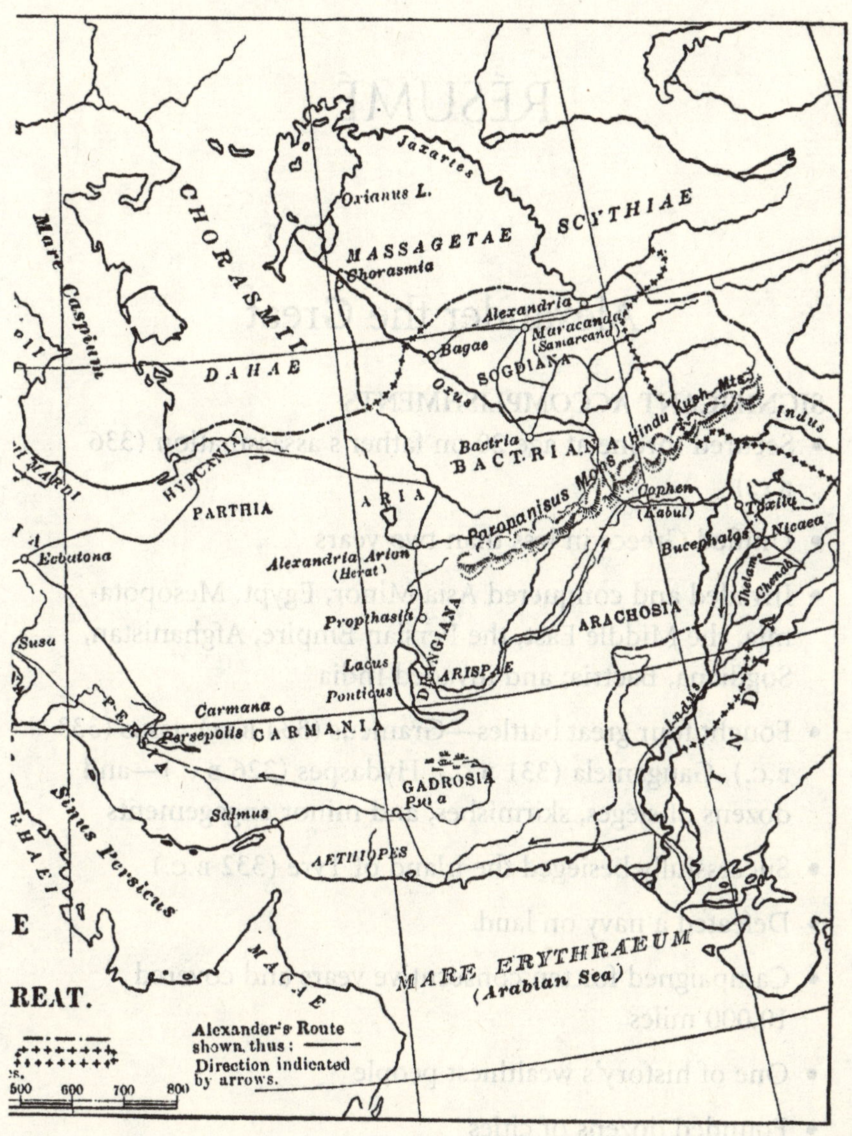
Jazartes
Oxianus L.
CHORASMII
MASSAGETAE
SCYTHIAE
Chorasmia
Mare Caspium
Alexandria
Maracanda
(Samarcand)
Bagae
DAHAE
SOGDIANA
Oxus
Hindu Kush Mts
Indus
Bactria
BACTRIANA
HYRCANIA
PARTHIA
ARIA
Paropanisus Mons
Cophen
(Kabul)
Taxila
Ecbatana
Alexandria Arion
(Herat)
Bucephalos
Nicaea
Jhelam
Chenab
Propthasia
ARACHOSIA
Susa
Lacus
Ponticus
ARISPAE
Carmana
Persepolis
CARMANIA
Indus
INDIA
GADROSIA
Salmus
Sinus Persicus
AETHIOPES
MARE ERYTHRAEUM
(Arabian Sea)
E
REAT.
Alexander's Route
shown thus:
Direction indicated
by arrows.
500 600 700 800

RÉSUMÉ

Alexander the Great

SIGNIFICANT ACCOMPLISHMENTS

- Secured throne at age 20 on father's assassination (336 B.C.)
- Unified Greece in less than two years
- Invaded and conquered Asia Minor, Egypt, Mesopotamia, the Middle East, the Persian Empire, Afghanistan, Sogdiana, Bactria; and invaded India
- Fought four great battles—Granicus (334 B.C.), Issus (333 B.C.), Gaugamela (331 B.C.), Hydaspes (326 B.C.)—and dozens of sieges, skirmishes, and minor engagements
- Successfully besieged the island of Tyre (332 B.C.)
- Defeated a navy on land
- Campaigned for ten consecutive years and covered 10,000 miles
- One of history's wealthiest people
- Founded dozens of cities
- Knew the names of 10,000 soldiers
- Wounded uncounted times, three times nearly fatally

PERSONAL NOTES

- Shared men's hardships; lived as a soldier
- Always fought visibly from the front
- Trained as a doctor and personally administered medical assistance to soldiers
- Always refused medical treatment (if conscious) before all others were treated, slept cold, ate sparingly

EDUCATION

Teachers: Leonidas (pre-adolescence), Aristotle (adolescence), Lysimachus (military)

Skills: King, history's greatest general, physician

Hobbies: Weapons, horses, geography, natural history, tactics

PERSONAL

Born: 356 B.C.—Pella, Macedonia

Family: Three wives—Parysatis (Persian princess), Stateira (oldest daughter of conquered Persian king, Darius III), and Roxane (Bactrian princess)—and one significant mistress (Barsine). All male heirs were murdered during wars of succession.

Hero: Homer

INTRODUCTION

The Four Leadership Processes

To allow you better to learn about leading—and about becoming a great leader—I have used four processes to organize some lessons that we can derive from Alexander the Great.[1]

I believe that leaders are in the reality creation business. They make the world, obviously within constraints, the way they want it to be. This is called *enactment*—the process whereby an actor takes an action, the outcome of which changes the world to which that actor subsequently responds. The actor, perhaps a leader, manager, parent, general, strategist, politician, coach, or thief, changes either the environment, situation, perceptions, rules, processes, ideas, or other like concepts. In all cases action is required.

1. For readers who would like to explore the theoretical ideas behind these processes, see Lance B. Kurke and Margaret Brindle, "The Process of Enactment: Evidence from Alexander the Great," in John Wagner (Ed.) *Advances in Qualitative Organizational Research*, Vol. 3 (Amsterdam: JAI, 2001), pp. 41–57.

In this book, I break down enactment—this reality creation activity—into four distinct processes that provide guidance to leaders: reframing problems, building alliances, establishing identity, and directing symbols. Each of these four activities is described in detail in its own chapter, where examples from Alexander's campaigns will provide specific, tangible examples.

CHAPTER 1

Leadership Process One: Reframing Problems

To reframe a situation is to change what people pay attention to or deem important. The meaning given to problems and the manner in which they are defined is critical. For example, by transforming an unsolvable task into another solvable one, the world to which we respond is essentially changed.

I believe that the most important job for leaders is to create reality for their organization. A fundamental way in which we do this is to frame and reframe problems presented to our organizations. For example, a good vision statement (e.g., the customer is first, quality is first, or employees are first) is a simple reframing that can transform the organization—provided customers, vendors, and employees behave differently because the statement is promulgated. This reframing occurs because the leader declares it or makes it so, which transforms reality. If quality comes first, there are implications for the value chain, the unions, the stockholders, and the customers that are different from the reality transformation derived from asserting that the customer comes first.

Alexander the Great sometimes reframed problems by creating another problem. When he solved this new, "created" problem, the original "unsolvable" problem was either irrelevant, trivial to solve, or moot. I call this process *problem displacement,* and it is arguably the most important leadership secret in this book. As you will see in the following historical analysis, Alexander the Great did not accept perceptions of his environment as limitations to be accommodated. Perceived problems were reframed into alternative problems, which were then solved. Often, the solution was to redefine the situation, and then act in accord with the newly constructed reality. The recast, solvable problem became the solution to the original problem. Sometimes just telling people something different from what they believed was enough.

1: Defeating a Navy on Land

Leaders are constantly confronted with "unsolvable" problems—those big, hairy, audacious problems that are intractable, even when you are throwing resources at them. My research suggests that the greatest leaders in history—military, political, and economic—do not attempt to solve such "impossible" problems when confronted with them. Rather, they find or create a different problem so that when they solve this new difficulty, the old unsolvable, or impossible problem becomes either trivial to deal with or irrelevant.

Alexander had fought and won two of his four great battles—Granicus and Issus—and was almost ready to penetrate to the core of the Persian Empire. First, however, he had to secure his needed supplies.

The food supply was his greatest challenge. Armies require enormous amounts of food, but in antiquity, commanders did not have the benefit of rapid-transit highways, helicopters, and large trucks to help them obtain it. Almost all food was transported in quantity by waterway. This meant that Alexander had to secure water routes from Greece to the coast and the rivers of Persia in order to be able to receive his supplies. Darius III, the Achaemenid king whose dynasty had controlled Persia for more than a thousand years, commanded a formidable navy of about 200 veteran warships. In contrast, Alexander had only a small coastal fleet and food-carrying barges. The problem was obvious: How could Alexander protect his food supply when the Persian navy could so blithely intercept the coastal barges?

The equally obvious answer would be to respond in kind by building a fleet. After all, that is what Julius Caesar did more than 300 years later when he needed to prevent the Veneti (modern-day low countries) from escaping their landside-encircled coastal fortresses. Caesar petitioned Rome for money and authorization to build the requisite fleet. However, Alexander could not build a fleet. He had neither the time nor the financial resources. His tenuous control of his army and homeland precluded the luxury of spending a year or two to locate resources and build a fleet. He would have needed trees cut down and cut up, mines mined, ores smelted, fittings manufactured, sails sewn, ropes made, and so on. He would have needed to captain and man 200 warships, train their crews, and provoke the Persians to confront him in a pitched battle. Then, he would have had to win that battle against a fleet of seasoned commanders. This direct approach to solving the problem was not a reasonable option. But what else could he do? (Stop. Think about your answer.)

The solution was so brilliant that it is studied today in every naval war college on the planet. Alexander was the first general to defeat a navy on land. Many have since tried to repeat this strategy. Some have succeeded, but he was the first.

How do you defeat a navy on land? Well, Alexander carefully gathered data until he completely understood his enemy—in this case, a fleet. This analysis revealed a key weakness: the need for fresh water. Today, we know nuclear submarines can go underwater and stay there for six months or more because reactor-driven desalination units distill salt water into fresh. In antiquity, though, distilleries could not create enough water to provision the crews. Plus, the fuel for a distillery was prohibitively heavy, and the fire hazard was enormous. As a result, naval commanders were constrained to carry their water with them, which put an upper bound on operating distances. Generally, these rowed vessels could carry a couple of days' supply of water for operating in the hot Mediterranean summer. A ship might either row out one day and back the next, or row out one day and continue on if the crew knew they could reach fresh water the next day. If Alexander's army secured all sources of fresh water within about two rowing days of his food barges' route, he could safeguard his supply.

While this may sound like a daunting task, Alexander managed it quite easily. His army garrisoned all sources of fresh water (e.g., rivers, wells, and lakes) or poisoned those sources they could not control or did not want to control. As the army marched down the coast of modern-day Lebanon, it came to the island city of Tyre. (Here we refer to new Tyre—the island—not old Tyre on the mainland, which was already as much as 500 years old.)

Tyre was critical to Alexander's plans. This region of the world has aquifers, and one of them supplied Tyre with unlimited fresh water. Tyre sold this water to the Persian fleet. But Tyre was impregnable. The island had survived being besieged for *thirteen years* by the Persian fleet. That is truly impregnable. The Tyrians were impossibly smug in their certainty that they were safe. Had they not been, they would not have responded as they did.

Before Alexander could move on, he had to control the water supply on Tyre, or convince the Tyrians not to sell fresh water to the Persian fleet. His first attempt was to approach the city leaders diplomatically (ostensibly to offer a sacrifice to the gods). He was impolitely rebuffed (some say he was veritably thrown off the island). This rejection of diplomacy left Alexander no choice. He set about besieging the city by land.

Yes—by land. He commanded his engineers and soldiers to build a mole over half a mile long (estimates range from five- to seven-tenths of a mile—call it a kilometer) and 100 to 200 yards wide. This causeway was simply a spit of land. Alexander's men all took up shovels and baskets, used some of the walls of old Tyre, found loose earth near the coast, loaded the baskets, and like an army of ants dumped their loads into the ocean. Gradually, they filled in the gap of water between the mainland and the city. This

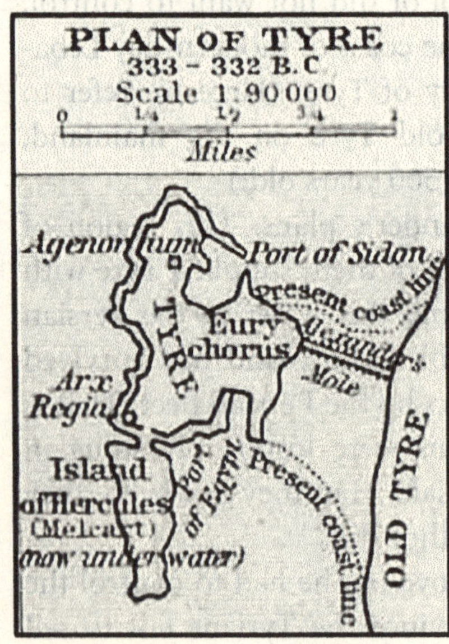

Alexander's reduction of Tyre was critical to his plans to conquer the Persian Empire. Source: *The Historical Atlas*, William R. Shepherd, New York, Henry Holt & Company, 1923. Courtesy of The General Libraries, The University of Texas at Austin.

process took about seven months. The Tyrians, of course, tried to stop this engineering marvel. Their fleet tried to destroy the work, and it almost succeeded, but Alexander's engineers built specialized towers and mobile battlements that protected the workers while they proceeded. He also borrowed small fleets to help guard the workers. When the causeway was complete, he was able to lay siege to the fortified island as though it were a city on land. It fell quickly—in about two weeks. The Tyrians were mostly slaughtered for their ill treatment of Alexander and their resistance. The Persian fleet was rendered ineffective. Alexander marched triumphantly on to Egypt.

Inferences and Allegations

Alexander looked at an island and saw, instead, land. He reconceived his problem so completely as to render pregnable what was impregnable. He reframed his problem from one of naval to one of earthly proportions. While such minds as his are rare, emulating them need not be.

Leading Lessons

As a leader, you are in the problem-reframing business. It is your job to create the reality to which the organization will devote its resources. You create this reality by identifying or creating other problems that are not unsolvable, so as to avoid deploying resources on problems that have no solution. In the previous illustration, Alexander immobilized the Persian fleet by taking away all its sources of fresh water. He reconceived an island as land, and built a mole to reach it. However, note that the alternative, reframed problem itself can be quite formidable.

Now stop and think about your most significant problem. Are you building a fleet to conquer Tyre (which is costly and time-consuming), or can you conceive of a causeway to reach it? What is your causeway? To recognize it, you need to know your strengths and use them, to know your weaknesses and avoid them, and to find your enemy's weaknesses and attack them.

U.S. Steel provides us with a modern example of problem reframing. The company had an environmental problem at one of its mills, where the residue of its coking operations (a high-pollution, necessary step in making steel) needed to be contained so as not to pollute the groundwater. The remediation was projected to be enormously expensive, and it could still fail. Many minds spent many months working to solve the containment problem. Then someone reframed the problem. By knowing the "strengths and weaknesses" of the situation, this problem reframer recognized that there was a small residual energy content in the waste. By mixing it in small amounts with the fuel for the furnaces, the company was able to eliminate the potential environmental problem by recasting it from containment to fuel. Fuel and remediation costs decreased, and the Environmental Protection Agency was happy.

When you encounter a problem, think of how it may be restructured into an opportunity to use your strengths or avoid your weaknesses. Doing this provides a greater opportunity for success, while allowing you to maximize (instead of waste) your resources.

2: Battle at the River Hydaspes

This lesson considers the task of defeating a much larger army that had war elephants, around which Alexander's cavalry would not fight. In antiquity, defeating an army possibly three times your size required a non-resource-based solution. In this case, Alexander reframed the problem. Instead of relying on military might, the solution rested on an elegantly choreographed use of the enemy's very strengths against them.

Toward the end of the decade-long campaign, Alexander fought the last of his four great battles near the western border of India, on the River Hydaspes, near the city of Haranpur.

Once Alexander got his army across the River Hydaspes (see Lesson 10), he faced an impossible task. The king opposing him, Porus, had a much larger army (outnumbering Alexander's by more than three to one) at a time when size almost always determined the outcome of a battle. (Until the invention of gunpowder, the larger army almost invariably defeated the smaller one by bringing more forces to bear at the point of contact. The exceptions to this rule are rare, and they are battles remembered by history precisely because of the mismatched sizes of the forces.) Porus also had 200 war elephants, an awesome force in those days. These elephants warrant our attention because they provide an invaluable lesson in leadership (and its twin, strategy).

Any reading of the literature surrounding Alexander shows that his cavalry was the key to his military prowess. He was a cavalry general, after all. Unfortunately, we have been deceived about horses and elephants all our lives. When we go to a circus and see these animals perform together, it is a misleading spectacle. Actually, horses have a natural, strong antipathy toward elephants. When a horse smells an elephant, it will attempt to throw its rider and gallop wildly away until it can no longer smell the other animal. This is true of both Asian and African elephants and all types of horses. When you see horses behaving controllably around elephants, it is because they have been raised to be comfortable with their smell. This is accomplished by putting the straw from an elephant's stable in with the colt from birth. By becoming acclimated, literally from birth, a horse can grow up to tolerate elephants.

All of Porus's horses were acclimated to elephants; none of Alexander's were. So, to compound the problem of defeating a superior-size army, Alexander did not have the use of his cavalry, which was usually the nucleus of his tactics, because Porus protected his infantry by odoriferously and strategically positioning the elephants.

Alexander marched his tired and exhausted army from the northernmost river crossing point to meet Porus's army to the south. Porus wisely reasoned that his army was fed and rested, whereas Alexander's was tired from marching all night, fighting a small battle at the crossing, and now marching through the mud to meet him. He picked a broad, level plain and waited there. Meanwhile, Alexander met segments of his army at prearranged crossings and provided them with secure passage across the river. By the time he met Porus, he had managed to get almost his entire army across safely.

The ensuing battle would have made a ballet choreographer proud. All leaders should so carefully plan their engagements. In preparation to meet this larger army, Alexander had drilled his troops to spread themselves out to the expected width of Porus's army. He thinned his ranks to about eight men deep. Porus's army was on the order of thirty or more men deep. Porus had reasoned that Alexander's ferocious cavalry would be the demise of his fine army, so he carefully organized his infantry so that the elephants were interspersed in front of or among the foot soldiers. This placement protected the Indians from Alexander's cavalrymen, who were riding elephant-fearing horses.

As a side note for the careful reader, we must consider the cavalry. Before the infantry battle began, Alexander had to figure out how to protect *his* troops from the enemy's cavalry. They were as vulnerable as Porus's troops would have been without benefit of the elephants' stench. Both armies stationed their cavalry on the wings—a standard disposition. Alexander had one of his cavalry generals, Coenus, feint in such a way that the Indian cavalry generals saw a splendid opportunity to capitalize on this "stupid" move and decimate the battalion. Coenus was actually bait. The battalion pretended to flee and was chased by all of the Indian cavalry, who saw a potential bloodbath. Actually, the feint worked as planned. Coenus stopped and reformed his battalion to meet the Indian cavalry charge. The other battalion of Alexander's cavalry now closed from behind, and the bloodbath consumed the surrounded Indians. Their cavalry was decimated, which secured the Greek army. This feint reframed the battle into an exclusively infantry battle.

To understand what happened next, we must digress and consider mahouts, sarissas, military police, mounted archers, and javelin throwers.

As you know, elephants are enormous, intelligent, long-lived mammals. They can be trained, but the trainer has to form a very special relationship with each animal. These trainers, with their special bonds to certain elephants, are called mahouts. At birth, a baby elephant is separated from its mother. From then on, the mahout provides all the food that baby elephant receives. He gives the elephant baths, brushes it, changes the straw in its stable (taking it to the horse stables), and very soon, certainly within days if not hours of the animal's birth, rides it by straddling its neck. Because elephants lived much longer than people did in Alexander's day, mahouts were selected for this lifelong job at a very young age—typically as young as five. (If the boy should be killed in the elephant's youth, the elephant was usually destroyed because no one else would ever be able to control the elephant. If the elephant died, the boy could not be reassigned to a different elephant, unless the boy was still very young.) At birth, elephants weigh about 250 pounds. One can picture a five-year-old boy climbing up on the baby elephant's neck and riding it. He would steer it by pulling on its ears. Even as the elephant grew to its 4,000- to 6,000-pound maturity, the mahout was able to control it because of their special bond. Each mahout was wedded to one elephant. Hold this image.

The Greek phalanxes were each equipped with a long, pike-like object called a sarissa. This pole could be of varying lengths, such that men, staggered in ranks of eight, could present a front of all their sarissas (or several of the front ranks). The distance from the Greek soldier to the sarissa's tip would have been carefully considered so that the length of the Indian soldier's arm, plus his stabbing sword, would be shorter, thus saving the Greek from injury. As a result, the front of Alexander's army became an impenetrable wall of steel points. Later, when the army marched to meet Porus's troops, it was able to contain the Indian front.

Because the Indian army consisted primarily of lightly trained peasant farmers who served only when needed, there was typically a great deal of desertion during battles. To combat this untimely departure of troops, it was almost certainly common practice to station military police in the back row of the army. This police force would likely consist of somewhat disabled veterans or older men who trained others during slack periods. This force would lock arms to keep desertion to a minimum. In the heat of battle, being as many as thirty rows back from the fray, the police force was probably oblivious to how things were going. Now we are prepared to examine the battle with the crucial mounted archers and javelin throwers.

In considering the start of the infantry battle, we must think of a ballet, as strange as that may sound. When the two armies were separated by just over a hundred yards, the mercenary Sogdian mounted archers that Alexander had hired (from modern Bukhara in Central Asia) came forward through passages in the infantry ranks. In antiquity, marksmen were archers. A good archer with a long bow could hit, say, a three- or four-inch target at about a hundred yards nine times out of ten. The Sogdian mounted archers could do this while riding. (Today, we are used to seeing movies wherein military snipers with laser scopes hit exact targets at up to two miles away with precise accuracy. But hitting a small target with an arrow nine times out of ten was quite a feat, especially when one considers the archer is riding a horse.) These archers rode to inside the edge of their range and systematically fired at their assigned targets. The first targets were the heads or chests of the mahouts. Given the numbers involved, the statistics, and the range, it must have been a very short time (twenty seconds at most?) before all the mahouts were dead. What could be an effective second target? Elephant eyes! As gruesome as this seems, the logic was impeccable. With each archer shooting at the elephant in front of him, in another minute, two at the very most, all of the elephants were without drivers and blind. As our "ballet" unfolded, the mounted archers quickly exited the battlefield. During the few minutes that they were engaged, Alexander's infantry marched ever closer to the Indian front with their wall of steel.

The javelin throwers came next. These men probably had a quiver of sorts to hold a number of javelins, perhaps as many as ten or fifteen. They were highly accurate at up to maybe fifty yards. Once they were in range, they released their load of weapons upon the hapless elephants directly in front of them. The javelin throwers now ran from the field. (John Maxwell O'Brien has the infantry using axes at close range, which would render equally horrific wounds.[1])

1. John Maxwell O'Brien, *Alexander the Great* (London: Routledge, 1992), p. 160.

The battle continued. At this precise moment, the front of Alexander's army arrived at the front of Porus's troops.

Picture the situation. The Indian soldiers are hemmed in by the Greeks and their wall of spear points in front, the military police in the back, hundreds of yards of fellow soldiers to the sides, and in their midst are the dreadfully wounded elephants. We now have 200 blind, driverless elephants writhing from the pain of having six-foot-long javelins buried up to one foot or more deep in their hides. What would you do in this situation if you were an elephant? Leave, of course. Thus, these two- to three-ton elephants stampeded among the Indians. The casualties resulted in one of the most lopsided victories in history. Alexander lost about 220 cavalrymen, ten mounted archers, and an insignificant number of infantry. Porus lost 4,000 cavalry and 21,000 infantry (9,000 killed outright and another 12,000 injured or captured).

Inferences and Allegations

Alexander reframed the hopeless problem of how to defeat an overwhelming opposing army such that the solution had the opposing army destroying itself. (Note that in complex situations, often more than one problem must be reframed.)

Leading Lessons

There are many lessons incumbent in the Battle at the River Hydaspes. Reframing problems requires very straightforward leadership skills, skills such as strategic and tactical planning. For example, most leaders seldom are wise enough to attack their competitors' weaknesses—relying instead on their own organization's strengths. But vulnerability can exist within either strength or weakness. Exploit your enemy's vulnerability. Conversely, understand your own vulnerabilities and protect them against exploitation.

A classic modern example was the corporate war waged between photographic film producers Eastman Kodak and Fuji Photo Film. Fuji beat Kodak in American markets by using its strength against it. Kodak reproduced perfect color. Fuji found that American consumers preferred color photos to be more toward the blue end of the spectrum, that is, imperfect. So Fuji manufactured film that produced this effect. Kodak retaliated in Japanese markets by attacking one of Fuji's greatest weaknesses—its distribution system. Kodak was able to sell its product at the many thousands of kiosks throughout the Japanese rail and subway system, bypassing normal distribution venues.

Remember: Reframe problems to exploit enemy weaknesses.

3: Suppressing the Revolt at Thebes

There are many ways to deal with disloyalty, revolt, or sedition. Each way may have exceedingly different effects on the people involved. In this situation, Alexander reframed a revolt: Instead of conquering a country, he won it through trust, and even friendship.

Very shortly after he became king of Macedonia, Alexander began campaigning in the northern part of modern-day Greece and adjacent regions, trying to secure his borders so that he could invade Persia without concern for his home base.

While he was campaigning in the north, the city of Thebes rebelled. It had been garrisoned by Macedonian troops (since the battle of Chaeronea in 338 B.C.), but disaffected exiles returned, killed the commanders, and led a full-scale revolt. Alexander recognized this as a central threat to the stability of all Greece and his future invasion of Persia. He dealt with it severely and marched quickly to Boeotia, the region in central Greece where Thebes is located.

The march was so speedy that the inhabitants of Thebes were unaware of Alexander's army until it was in their midst. Rapidity of movement was one of Alexander's hallmarks. The army encamped, besieged, and conquered the citadel. So far, this was a straightforward suppression of the revolt.

The aftermath is noteworthy and as important as the chalice at the altar. Alexander acted as the Hegemon of the

Unifying various Greek city-states and alliances provided Alexander the base of support for all his subsequent campaigns. Source: *The Historical Atlas*, William R. Shepherd, New York, Henry Holt & Company, 1923. Courtesy of The General Libraries, The University of Texas at Austin.

League of Corinth—not as Macedonian king. (The League was a loose and heretofore relatively ineffective alliance created by Alexander's father, Philip II.) Alexander allowed the League to decide the fate of Thebes, and it made a highly punitive decision, partly out of jealousy and partly out of greed. Many Thebans were massacred, although there were some notable exceptions. The city was razed. The survivors were sold into slavery. The land was distributed to the members of the League of Corinth. This extreme punishment of Thebes shocked the rest of Greece into coalescence with Alexander's hegemony over the League. It also had the effect, specifically, of intimidating Athens. The Athenians expected their city to be sacked. Sparing Athens changed Alexander's image from a conqueror who was not to be trusted to a unifier, worthy of alliance.

So efficacious was the heavy-handed treatment of Thebes—by the League, not Alexander—that all of Greece sent emissaries to Alexander, both to congratulate him and to win his indulgence. He took some hostages and accepted the locals' punishments of those siding with Thebes or inspiring it to revolt. By stopping his conquest (which was almost certainly within his grasp) here, Alexander was able to secure a home base of allies, not subjected city-states, while he resumed his father's aborted invasion of Persia.

Inferences and Allegations

Alexander's original problem was how to secure Macedonia's borders and pacify Greece, presumably through conquest, as his father had tried to do for decades. Alexander was able to reframe the problem so that it resulted in unity, not conquest. This solution was brilliant, but it is rarely emulated today during acquisitions.

Leading Lessons

Victory can be defined in various ways. Some victories are of more long-term value than others are. By *not* conquering Athens, and by employing an extra-organizational agency effectively, Alexander could safely leave the country without fear of subsequent revolt.

A failed example comes to mind. When US Airways acquired Piedmont Airlines (for access to the Charlotte, North Carolina, hub), it acquired an airline with one of the finer flight service groups in the industry. This acquisition occurred during a time when US Airways had a reputation for poor in-flight service. An appropriate reframing would have turned this acquisition to its advantage and allowed the former Piedmont leaders to implant their service standards throughout the new, merged airline. Unfortunately, for reasons that are not public, all significant Piedmont executives affiliated with flight attendant recruiting, selection, training, and so on left the merged organization within just a few months. Conquest was harmful to service in the long term. Unity, with the subsequent appearance of loss of control, would have been a better way to reframe the situation.

4: On Possessions

One of the most important military tenets is mobility. For thousands of years, mobility and its offspring, flexibility, have been constant sources of strategically and tactically based victories (as opposed to resource-based victories of overwhelming numerical or technological superiority). Alexander won several battles and engagements by getting to a geographically or tactically significant point first. Typically, the loss of mobility is addressed by adding more transport, more horsepower, double-time demands of soldiers, earlier departures, etc. (Modern equivalents include outsourcing, overtime, hiring temporary workers, and backstopping half-baked product launches.) Alexander reframed his loss of mobility.

By the time Alexander headed east toward present-day Afghanistan, having accepted the head of Darius III (the Achaemenid king; see Chapter 3, Lesson 25) and the Persian kingship, his army had collected plundered wealth on a scale unimaginable to the Greek soldiers. Indeed, the army had an extra wagon train to transport its bounty. Thus, the army had lost much of its mobility.

While probably an exaggeration, it is said the common soldiers, who would decamp at daybreak, were so burdened that when the vanguard approached a new camping spot, the tail was still decamping. Alexander's army was supposed to be mobile. It had gotten rich. It had grown fat. It had gotten slow.

Alexander summoned all his soldiers and made a compelling speech about the need for mobility. Afterward, in front of his men, he torched his own wagons with his take of the plunder, sparing only the quartermaster's supplies (including bullion for pay) and ambulances. He who had the most to lose went first, and he bade his followers to follow.

They did.

The army regained its mobility from the ashes.

Inferences and Allegations

Alexander brooked no distinction in rank when it came to his military obligations. He endured no exceptions. He led from the front—especially in combat—by example.

Leading Lessons

Be fair. Don't be obsessed with possessions. Take forceful steps to deal with problems. Use symbolism as appropriate (see Chapter 4). These are all important lessons, but here I wish to emphasize the role of reframing problems. Alexander did *not* try to solve the mobility problem with the traditional solution of slack resources. Rather, he reconceived of his army as it had been in the beginning: small, mobile, and flexible. The way to regain this initial formulation was to recreate it from the flames. Despite the hard-fought fights to acquire wealth, the army gladly reduced it to ashes when asked to do so by a great leader who knew how to make the request visually (by example), symbolically (with fire), and personally (by going first).

Modern positive equivalents are rare, but negative examples are commonplace. The Japanese have a well-earned, deserved reputation for greater fairness in compensation than most other advanced economies. The highest-paid executives earn only a fraction of what their U.S. counterparts do. And when the economy takes a downturn or the company performs badly, it is the executives, not the hourly or union people, who take the cuts. In America, it is commonplace for an executive to fly in by corporate jet or helicopter, take a limousine to the meeting hall, and explain that the employees must make sacrifices (with layoffs, income reductions, pension cutbacks, or benefits slashes). This empty "leadership" from behind is not remotely in league with the great leaders in history.

5: On Founding Cities

Alexander faced a problem greater than any leader in ancient history—how to hold a new empire together without adequate military resources to properly garrison it. No one before or since (except possibly the Soviet Union in the twentieth century) set out to integrate so many cultures, both eastern and western. Alexander's solution was to reframe the problem—creating as many as seventy cities and towns. (Other solutions are discussed in Chapter 4.)

Alexander had two recurring problems: what to do with the wounded, the sick, the lame, the old, and the veterans whose appointments expired, and how to control conquered lands.

Alexander's solution was to set up tactical military outposts, peopled by a combination of wounded Macedonian veterans (or those whose draft had expired), camp followers, local volunteers, and a small garrison. They were always located with good water, good land, and strategic military value. Some of them—for example, Alexandria in Egypt—were to become world centers. A few of the cities he founded (such as the city named after his horse where it died) were tokens to his ego.

Inferences and Allegations

Alexander solved the problem of treating veterans justly by leaving a core collection of veterans (usually slightly wounded) with some locals and giving them land. He solved the problem of controlling conquered territories by founding cities for these veterans at strategically significant sites.

Leading Lessons

Recent history often shows modern organizations casting off many employees. Sometimes this decision is called early retirement, downsizing, rightsizing, layoffs, or anything else. Great leaders might do better to emulate Alexander and find creative solutions to their business problems. Except perhaps in situations of industry overcapacity, companies could create new subsidiaries that would operate at arm's length, peopled by executives and employees who might own some of the new entity. Given time to perform, the subsidiary might become a valuable entity or be worthy of sale, whether to others or to the employees themselves. This type of action can solve multiple problems, such as reducing a too-high headcount, eliminating "executive dumping grounds," and potentially creating greater corporate wealth, while treating employees with dignity and benefiting society.

The flip side of this kind of action is that too many modern leaders can expand their empires for all the wrong reasons. Executives acquire companies ostensibly for strategic reasons, but later, they may realize the lack of fit and cast off their predecessors' toys. Why do executives do such things? Well, one common reason is that executive retirement packages are tied to stock price, which is correlated with gross sales, so any sales, even those in illogical industry segments, help to enlarge "golden parachutes." Another reason is the desire by executives to leave a legacy. Leaders control enormous organizational resources, and they can direct those resources to almost any end that can be justified to the board. But legacies are usually measured in size, not quality. Why can't a legacy create a core competency that will make the organization a mean competitor for decades to come, rather than a jigsaw agglomeration of mismatched acquisitions? Ponder your legacy before you act.

6: Mutiny

No leader has penultimate power. No employee has unlimited endurance. No army can do more than the synergy provided by the individual soldiers. When an army revolts, leaders can do many things: punish with extreme discipline (for example, shooting deserters or flogging those who disobey), reward with huge bonuses (Alexander did this often, and it was a common Roman practice), admonish, or even beg (a common modern practice). Alexander got away with redefining reality by reframing mutiny and turning it into *his* decision to go home.

After the battle at the River Hydaspes, Alexander continued further into the Punjab, intending, apparently, to defeat all of India. Rumors were that he might even go to China. The troops refused to go on.

Imagine: They were thousands of miles from home. They had been campaigning almost continuously for eight years, and they had seen many of their comrades killed or wounded. They had suffered disease, deprivation, and hunger. They had walked several thousand miles and had yet to walk back. And, they lived in near constant fear for their lives. Enough was enough, and nothing Alexander said would change their minds.

Alexander disappeared into his tent for three days, not seeing anyone. Then he emerged from his meditations to announce that *he* had decided that the army was going home. He recognized defeat, and he turned it into a victory by declaring it so.

Inferences and Allegations

While it is true that Alexander petulantly sulked in his tent for three days (an action that is not very statesmanlike), he used the time to reframe this defeat into a victory simply by reversing roles. He turned the army's decision into his decision; therefore, there was no mutiny. However, he was not seen to be backing down, either. Essentially, this is an example of "saying it is so makes it so."

Leading Lessons

No matter who you are, no matter what your cause, no matter how great a leader you are, it is possible to push your troops too far, to expect too much, to demand more than can be given.

A leader understands the capabilities and limitations of employees. The former president of my employer, Duquesne University, promulgated the vision of becoming the number-one Catholic university in America. No time constraints were given. No measurement criteria were outlined. No guidance as to how this would happen was provided. Of course, such a goal is nearly impossible given, for example, Notre Dame's billion-dollar endowment. A decade or so later, this president declared victory, citing numerous criteria (for example, Duquesne was the most-wired, best-education-for-the-money institution). Even though few competitors would proffer the number-one slot to the university, our leader said it was so, making it so in the eyes of employees, students, alumni, foundations, and donors.

7: Trust and Loyalty

On occasion Alexander was betrayed. He dealt ruthlessly with the Persians and other kings and rulers, but was more hesitant when dealing with Greeks.

By late in the decade-long campaign, Alexander seemed to grow more suspicious. Parmenion was one of his father's most trusted advisers, and he had remained most helpful to Alexander. Parmenion's son, Philotas, accompanied Alexander on the entire campaign, while the father was given an important administrative post at Ecbatana, guarding the royal treasury.

Parmenion and Philotas. Father and son. Trustworthy and loyal. One unfairly murdered upon orders from Alexander, the other possibly unfairly executed because of complicity with conspiracy.

Philotas was executed because he had knowledge of a conspiracy to murder Alexander, but he did not report it to him. When the conspiracy was uncovered, Philotas was guilty by association—for *not* acting when he felt it was an empty threat. Once all the conspirators were dead, it apparently occurred to Alexander that Philotas's father might have been guilty of conspiracy as well (although it seems unlikely). Or, perhaps Parmenion was executed because of jealousy—he was enormously popular with the army. Whether guilty by association or out of jealousy, Parmenion was killed before news of the conspiracy reached the army. (Alexander had dispatched the orders for his execution by racing camel, no less.) Upon Parmenion's death, the army nearly mutinied. The troops who expressed support for him, or those who wrote letters home that were negative about Alexander, were grouped together in a "disciplinary company" to avoid infecting the rest of the troops.

Inferences and Allegations

One might argue that this story does not demonstrate greatness, but perhaps just paranoia. Alexander may have made a bad decision here, and perhaps this story belongs in a section on "Lesser Moments." However, the fallout of the possibly bad decision is where the lesson lies. The troops might have mutinied because of their high loyalty to Parmenion.

Leading Lessons

If you have to make unpopular decisions, and "mutiny" or sabotage is a possibility, decide in advance how to contain the damage. Unhappy workers are an infection that can cause lingering damage. If some employees do not respond to efforts to win them over, they may become like a virus and spread their discord. People who clearly will never be won over should be weeded out. Organizations do this all the time, whether by co-opting key union leaders by bringing them into management, selling a piece of the organization to top management, or other practices.

A classic modern example is Winton Blount's handling of the old Post Office Department during the Nixon administration. Blount had a congressional and presidential mandate to make the department efficient. He knew that unions, entrenched management, congressional patronage, organizational culture, traditions, and so on would guarantee failure of large-scale, systemic change. His solution was pervasive. While he offered to include everyone, he fired those who clearly were not in accord with the new culture—even though this was many thousands of people. He changed the name of the organization to the U.S. Postal Service. He brought in MBAs from industries that employed efficient processes. A massive infusion of technology was imposed upon the union. A newsletter bombarded the remaining employees with a consistent barrage of information about efficiency, new technologies, and various measures of success. The thoroughly well planned change was carefully promulgated to the culture of hundreds of thousands of postal workers. When instituting mass change, especially when it involves gaining the trust and loyalty of employees, plan for the need to eliminate the untrustworthy, convert the amenable, and leverage the zealots.

8: How to Capture an Impregnable Stronghold

The definition of the problem is often the problem. If a rock is impregnable, then it is because we agree in advance that it is. Perception is usually reality.

After becoming the de jure and de facto king of the Persian Empire, Alexander set off to the east to secure the scurrilous hill tribes. These tribes had bedeviled the Persians for centuries. They remained outside the mainstream, often being "subdued," only to rise up again when the visiting army had departed. They always had their citadel to retreat to—the Rock of Aornos.

The Rock of Aornos was considered impregnable, and thus it was a refuge for the many locals who fled Alexander's wrath and mayhem during his transit through the region west of the Indus River. All the descriptions of it, as well as its extraordinary siting, make it seem as truly impregnable as legend had it.

The legend was that even the son of Zeus, Heracles, had failed to capture Aornos. Of course, this meant that Alexander *had* to capture it. While he set up to conquer and hold all surrounding towns, he began a standard siege. Everyone, it appears, was convinced of the invincibility of the rock. And it was invincible—unless Alexander could convince his army otherwise.

The key to solving this problem was a nearly impossible "flanking movement" that would be done by scaling the sheer walls on one side of the rock. (Local guides had revealed this sheer cliff to Alexander.) That flank was never defended because it was believed no one could scale it. Wrong. The scaling of the rock by Alexander's troops was so unexpected that it succeeded. It is worth brief note that Alexander's human resources capabilities were renowned, so he could call upon his army, with proper inducements, and they would deliver.

Inferences and Allegations

Alexander did not accept the apparent reality presented to him. Ever. An impregnable location obviously wasn't, because Alexander was Alexander *the Great.* He reframed any and all "unsolvable" problems. Here, he recognized that the *perception* of impregnability was the very weakness of the entrenched army.

Leading Lessons

Saying it is so sometimes makes it so. In my experience, leaders are often their own worst enemy. Because they cannot conceive of some outcomes, they cannot possibly achieve them. I often train executives about fire walking (the practice of walking barefoot over a long bed of burning coals, a practice recognized worldwide but uncommon in America, and therefore incorrectly believed to be impossible without harming the feet). Exposure to fire walking often opens the realm of possibility. Alexander seemed never to have such closed realms.

About 1990, Jack Welch wanted General Electric (GE)

to double its revenues from roughly $100 billion in a decade. The problem was that when he asked all his strategic business unit (SBU) managers to project what they could expect to contribute to this growth, the total numbers came up to only about $40 billion in additional sales. The problem turned out to be only conceptual; the problem was one of Welch's own definition. Around 1980, Welch demanded the business units be number one or two in their industry, or they would be divested. All GE's SBUs had to take market share away from other market giants, thus severely limiting growth because of the intense competition between economic giants. The solution, proposed by an army colonel at a breakout session, was to *redefine* each industry segment. Thus, industry segments defined as glues could become adhesives, lightbulbs became lighting, sandpaper became abrasives, etc. These industry redefinitions enlarged the market and permitted far greater growth. This reframing enabled GE to become one of the largest industrial concerns in the world. Again, leaders' perceptions and beliefs can be the problem. Change your perceptions and beliefs.

9: Logistics Is Underappreciated

A common modern solution to logistical problems is to throw more resources at them. If supplies are interdicted, send more supplies. If the market is not meeting expectations, spend more on advertising. If material is not produced fast enough, buy more machines, or add a shift. These resource-based solutions do get the job done. But at what expense? Alexander commonly reframed his problems to be less resource based.

Provisioning his army, especially with food, was a problem throughout his lengthy campaign, but it was especially trying before he conquered the administrative heartland of the Persian Empire. Usually Alexander could acquire food from Greece or, later, Egypt. But often he had to acquire food locally, and he did not want to steal it from the locals because he wanted to "rule" benevolently. After he became king of Persia, the task got much easier, except at places like the Gedrosian Desert.

Food could have created a very different outcome, maybe even relegating Alexander to a historical footnote to his rightly famous father, who essentially invented the modern army. Had the satraps (the royally appointed governors) at Granicus (Alexander's first great battle) laid waste to the countryside ahead of Alexander, it might have precluded his further incursion, because in the beginning, Alexander had very few possessions, very little support, and limited transport capabilities. Unfortunately, these noble appointees of Darius felt that combat, not the ignoble burning of crops, was the way to handle the Greeks (whom the

Persians held in contempt). Greed may also have induced the local satraps to fight, instead of burn crops (since they would lose taxes if all the crops were burned). In the beginning, it is probable that not even Alexander's logistical machine could have supported the invasion.

In contrast to what happened at Granicus, shortly after the death of Darius, Bessus (a deposed Persian nobleman) challenged Alexander by declaring himself king, gathering troops from Bactria and other allies. Bessus continued to retreat from Alexander's overwhelmingly powerful army, burning crops as he retreated, eventually crossing the Oxus River (the modern northern boundary of Afghanistan) into what was then called Sogdiana. (Incidentally, this was the region where Alexander hired the mounted archers who played such a significant role in the battle at the River Hydaspes.) Alexander and his army crossed the Hindu Kush (one of the world's most imposing mountain ranges). Although this was a very formidable accomplishment in its own right, the army went on to subdue Bactria (where Alexander later met and married Roxane), and then swiftly followed Bessus across the Oxus.

Inferences and Allegations

Eventually, Bessus's allies realized that they faced the same fate as Darius, whose death Bessus had engineered. Appropriately, the allies arrested Bessus and turned him over to Alexander—alive, naked, and in a wooden collar. His fate is told in several stories. We do not know which one is correct, but they are all unpalatable and even gruesome. For example, some say his nose and ears were cut off, and then he was returned to Darius's family, who dispatched him in a very slow, intensely painful butchering that concluded with small pieces of his body being spread across the countryside. Another lovely story is that he was tied to two trees that had been bent down. When the restraints were removed, Bessus was torn in half. Other stories are equally vivid. It does not matter what actually happened. What matters is that the fate of Bessus further made it clear to the people of the empire that Alexander was king and that he would deal not only with disloyalty but with any attacks on his food supply.

Leading Lessons

Alexander correctly reframed the problem from one of provisioning supplies to foraging the enemy. He repeatedly captured the Persian supplies intact.

More than 3,000 years ago, Sun Tzu admonished all would-be generals to forage the enemy. Alexander sought not to alienate the civilians by stealing their food, so he set out to capture enemy baggage and supplies. Forage the enemy.

Conversely, burn your competitors' crops as a way to reduce competition. A modern example is the common practice of ruining competitors' test marketing or product introductions. When a competitor brings a new product into your market, give away or dramatically reduce the price of your comparable product, buy extensive end-aisle displays, distribute coupons, buy advertising to drown out the competitor's launch, or use some combination of these tactics. This is the equivalent of burning crops because the consumer will respond to your tactics and buy your product. The result is that the competitor has a poor launch—possibly even pulling the new product because of disappointing results—or gets essentially no accurate data about the product because all of your actions skew the results. In all cases, very rapid, decisive action is required.

10: Crossing the River Hydaspes

Near the end of ten years of campaigning, Alexander faced Porus, a king in India, at the River Hydaspes, which was turbulent and would drown unprepared soldiers laden with heavy armor and weapons. Normally, horses would help infantry cross a river because horses are such excellent swimmers. Recall, however, that the far side was defended not just by an overwhelmingly bigger army, but by elephants, whose scent kept Alexander's cavalry at bay. Brute force could not produce a crossing. The problem had to be reframed—the original problem displaced.

Before the battle at the River Hydaspes, Alexander had to cross this powerful tributary of the River Indus—the major river that drained all of the western Himalayas. This river will catch your arm and drag you downstream to your death.

Upon arriving at the riverbank, Alexander had his men establish camp, and the very next morning, he took half the army and marched up the river. Porus, the king and general of the local Indians, had no choice but to take half of his army and march opposite Alexander's army to deter a crossing. By midday, Alexander stopped for lunch and then returned to camp. Porus's army did the same. The next day, Alexander's army marched down the river (to further reconnoiter a possible ford). Porus had to follow to make sure Alexander did not cross. Porus followed the army opposite him when it returned to camp. This went on for day after day, week after week, maybe month after month.

One can imagine that at some point, an Indian soldier pointed out the obvious: "The River Hydaspes cannot be crossed in the face of our opposition. Alexander is keeping his army fit and disciplined until the fall and winter, when the snows gather in the Himalayas and the river will be easier to cross. Thus, it is unnecessary to march opposite the enemy every day. We have identified all possible fords and can simply garrison them with soldiers or cavalry—for rapid message communication, in case they do try to cross—and an elephant, whose smell will keep their cavalry from crossing." The Indian officer corps agreed, and they garrisoned all the fords. This is exactly what Alexander wanted. He wanted Porus to relax his vigilance. Only with a relatively unimpeded crossing could Alexander get the army across.

The crossing itself was simple and clever. The army had actually been practicing marching silently. Each unit had learned to pad its armor and weapons, so as to make no noise. The army also reconnoitered a path that let the men march north without being seen. On the night of the subterfuge crossing, the army split in two, with those marching doing so in silence. Because marching armies produce clouds of dust, Alexander chose a night that had torrential rain, to further reduce the Indian army's anxiety about a possible night crossing. Finally, he would have insisted that the same number of fires be burned, in keeping with the normal routine. A large allocation of alcohol for those remaining at Alexander's camp would keep the men's spirits up and voices loud, so the Indians would observe the same number of fires and about the same level of noise as the full army, and have no idea that half of the unit was missing. Some sources say a decoy, disguised as Alexander, paraded around ostentatiously, but this seems improbable given the need to choose a rainy night to cover the dust.

The marching army unintentionally crossed to an island, not immediately realizing this mistake. Eventually they crossed over the river, using inflated goatskins or small, straw-filled rafts for extra flotation, to help offset the weight of the armor and weapons. Alexander's army then fought the local garrison, killed the sole elephant stationed there for its smell as quickly as possible, and buried it. Then his men brought the horses over. Alexander's army had the advantage of perhaps 200 collapsible boats. The commander of the Indian cavalry (composed of a few hundred horses), one of Porus's sons, was killed in the skirmish.

Inferences and Allegations

A crossing is not merely a crossing. A crossing is an opportunity to lull the enemy into a false sense of security, so you don't have to fight at a serious disadvantage. Marching up and down the river and not attempting to cross in the beginning was a ploy to reinforce the plausible inference that Alexander was waiting until winter. This reframed the problem from one of force to the cognitive solution of subterfuge.

Leading Lessons

When engaged with the enemy in corporate war, it sometimes helps to wait until the enemy lets its guard down. A modern example is that of the recent battle between Polaroid and a competitor that introduced a camera that took quick-developing pictures in direct competition with Polaroid's traditional market of instant film and cameras. Rather than immediately seeking an injunction against the competitor for what it knew to be patent violations, Polaroid patiently waited until the product was well established in the market, and then it sought a court injunction. Polaroid eventually won in court, receiving a billion-dollar settlement, and the competitor had to withdraw the product from the market. If you hold the high ground, let the enemy begin its attack. As Sun Tzu said, put yourself in a position from which you cannot be defeated, and then wait for the enemy to provide the opportunity to defeat it.

11: Conservative Advice Forsaken

Who shall receive your blessing upon your retirement or death? How good is your organization at succession planning? When Alexander ascended to the throne, he had no heir. Councilors advised caution: Take a wife, have children, guarantee a potential heir. However, Alexander felt that taking action—invading Persia—was more important. The risk was chaos if Alexander was killed.

Macedonian kingship was an "elected" post. Heirs did not automatically become king, but had to gain the approval of the army, although sons of the king did have high expectations of being elevated to the throne. So, if Alexander left no heir, Macedonia would face awful turmoil.

During the period immediately before Alexander crossed the Hellespont to invade Persia, preparations were undertaken to support the Persian campaign. Traditionally, the king sought counsel of the nobility. One historical source (Diodorus) says that two of Philip's (Alexander's father) most important advisers, Antipater and Parmenion, strongly encouraged Alexander to find a spouse and ensure an heir before he left for what might become a lengthy campaign. Of course, if he were killed, the succession would be contested.

Alexander was a rather impatient young man (except at places such as Tyre, where he was supremely patient) and impetuous (and continued to be throughout his campaigns). The advice, to a young man, seemed impossibly cautious, and it was rejected outright. Waiting for years was inconceivable to a young man hell-bent on invasion.

Inferences and Allegations

Alexander reframed the problem of succession: Instead of accepting only a Macedonian heir, any heir from *any* princess acceptable to Alexander could succeed him. He could not *say* this, of course, for fear of losing favor at court while he was away. Alexander showed that succession might be important, but he refused to hold up the invasion to guarantee it. Heirs could be found on the campaign—something that the xenophobic Greek noblemen had not anticipated. Marrying a barbarian who would provide an heir was unthinkable.

Leading Lessons

Unorganized action is preferable to organized inaction. Sometimes leaders listen to subordinates or trusted confidants who may have seldom, if ever, been wrong. Sometimes it is prudent to wait—to listen to the counsel of counselors. But many times we seek reports, we want market studies, or, to bolster our own insecurities, we demand that risk be reduced, which is often an illusion. It has become obvious that excellent companies often act precipitously.

A prime product example of this lesson is Rubbermaid. At its peak, while it was still a stand-alone company, Rubbermaid was introducing 300 new products per year, with a 90 percent success rate, when its competition had a 10 percent success rate with a fraction of the new product launches. The reason Rubbermaid was so successful for so long was precisely because it did not follow standard marketing routines: focus groups, test marketing, and all the rest. The company encouraged its design engineers who thought of an injection-molded plastic product that they would use at home or anywhere else to create that product and launch it with the torrential flood of other new products. Rubbermaid's unorganized action was preferable to organized inaction.

Related to the selection of heirs is the modern human resources example of succession planning, which is not a last-minute process. Often we do not know who would be the best replacement. Commonly, we reframe the decision from selecting the leader to selecting the front-runners who compete in a leadership tournament. One lesson is to expeditiously select who will compete in that tournament. (Conversely, announcing succession too far in advance can have negative effects: eliminating constructive competition, losing valuable also-rans, and, occasionally, insurrection.)

Concluding Thoughts on Reframing Problems

By now, I hope you appreciate the extraordinary power of reframing problems. When confronted with a seemingly unsolvable problem, you can reframe the problem, solve that new problem, and eliminate the original problem. I call this *problem displacement.* This technique has been in use for thousands of years, but it has never been studied systematically or popularized. Obviously, it does not work in every situation. But when resources are inadequate, the goals too grand, or the time constraint too short, these are indicators that maybe *you* are the problem, because you have accepted the definition of the problem.

Notice the range of actions Alexander the Great used in reframing situations: choreographing the battle (at the River Hydaspes); using the enemy's strength against them (elephants); adjusting simple technology (the length of sarissas); using extra-organizational agencies (the League of Corinth); not destroying the enemy in order to make them an ally (Athens); burning the wagons (to gain mobility); founding cities (to create security and retirement communities); redefining mutiny (as when Alexander said that going home was his idea); looking at the sea and seeing land (at Tyre); foraging the enemy (everywhere); using deception (to cross the River Hydaspes); and acting without organizing (initiating the invasion of Persia without an heir). In hindsight, the outcomes almost seem inevitable. They were not. Success came from Alexander's amazing ability to reframe problems. How, you might ask, can you use such a simple range of actions to rout your competitor? This is a good question indeed.

Reframing and problem displacement are powerful tools in planning at any level of an organization. The first step in a strategic, tactical, or functional plan is to be clear about the objectives, whether we call this the vision, mission, objective, or goal. If we conceive of goals that are too modest, we may achieve them, and everybody will be happy. But we may have left too much money on the table. A grander conception might have served the organization fantastically.

A common barrier to successful reframing is the leader's ability to conceive. There is a well-known principle that if you can conceive, and you can believe in your conception, then you can achieve it. The idea is that great leaders are able to conceive of things that others may find inconceivable, such as the women's movement, the environmental movement, the development of laptop or handheld computers, or space planes, the elimination of poverty, or the goal of world peace. If it can be conceived, and the leader is convinced of its authenticity, its capability for being brought into existence, and its rightness, then it can be achieved. The converse is simple. If you cannot conceive of something, your organization is highly unlikely to achieve it. Conceiving, believing, and achieving are critical to reframing. Without them, achievement is impossible. My experience is that people and organizations are capable of much more than many leaders realize. In such cases, leaders become the barrier. They stifle the organization. Don't be the problem. Conceive the solution, believe it, and achieve it.

CHAPTER 2

Leadership Process Two: Building Alliances

Building strong alliances via reciprocity has become a critical strategy for modern leaders. Similarly, the effective and deliberate construction of alliances was also extremely important to ancient leaders. Alexander formed alliances throughout his life—seamlessly building important relationships with individuals, organizations, cities, and peoples. These alliances changed the world to which he subsequently responded. At some level, one can argue that Alexander was a conqueror, pure and simple. However, on numerous occasions, alliances were preferred over conquests, as was co-opting the enemy instead of destroying it.

12: Aftermath of the Battle at the River Hydaspes

It is hard today to imagine how diverse the Persian Empire was. Holding it together, especially as he was enlarging it, was a formidable challenge for Alexander. The Persians had never been able to provide a secure border with India except through unstable military truces.

The strategic situation after the defeat of Porus, the Indian king, completely changed the potential eastern boundaries. Never before had the Persians won a significant victory against the Indians.

Porus had just witnessed the decimation of his army. He lost two or three sons. His kingdom was clearly lost to him without his army. He was wounded. As a mahout, he rode his elephant away with unimaginable feelings of failure and loss. He must have been quite a sight: tall, reportedly extremely handsome, dark, bearded, riding a white elephant. Alexander, seeing him ride away, gathered up some Indian horses that could operate around elephants and chased the defeated king. Alexander caught up with Porus, stopped him, and confronted him with a question. There is disagreement over the exact question, but whatever it was, Porus's answer deeply impressed Alexander. Imagine one version of this conversation: Alexander asks, "How shall I treat you?" Porus, with great aplomb, answers, "Kill me, or treat me as the king I am." (Note that Porus does not use the past tense *was.*) Another version has Alexander asking what to do with Porus, who answers, "I am king." Asked further what he wants, Porus replies that the word *king* contains all the information Alexander needs. In either scenario, Alexander was so taken by Porus's answer and demeanor (whatever it was) that he promised him his kingdom intact—and he even enlarged it. So beholden was Porus that his heirs remained loyal to Alexander's successors for generations.

Inferences and Allegations

Alexander reframed the situation from having to occupy the conquered lands to having an important ally. This created the most enduring alliance to come out of his entire campaign.

Leading Lessons

"The quality of mercy is not strained, it droppeth as the gentle rain from heaven upon the place beneath. . . ."[1] A convert often becomes a vocal supporter. Whether the convert is a reformed alcoholic, a religious convert, or someone who discovers the power of lean manufacturing or continuous quality improvement, he can become a zealot. Zealots can change the world. How can modern leaders create zealots? The Japanese-style commitment to lifelong employment, the generous benefits program of Ben and Jerry's, the extremes to which Nike goes for its corporate employees, and the social benefits enjoyed by many European workers

1. William Shakespeare, *The Merchant of Venice*, Act IV. Sc. 1.

have all created zealots. These examples are also demonstrations of leadership. Giving budding leaders who made an honest mistake, but who clearly learned from it, a second chance is another opportunity to exhibit great leadership. This type of magnanimity and trust creates loyalty out of indifference. Bringing leaders into the corporate fold after an acquisition or merger, when they expect to be cast off or marginalized, also creates zealots of them, but may alienate others who desire those very jobs.

13: Royal Hostages

How to handle acquisitions is a critical question, debated by the likes of Sun Tzu and Machiavelli. Do you crush or nurture? Do you adopt or banish? Sometimes distinctive or distinguished acquisitions come our way in the form of human resources.

Alexander routed the Persian army at Issus, his second great battle, on the coast where the Anatolian highlands meet Phoenicia. After the battle at Issus, the army captured the Persian baggage train carrying all the royal possessions and Darius's family. The hostages included the king's wife, mother, harem, numerous slaves, and household items. The options available to Alexander included, at least, the following. He could have treated the family as property, turning them over to the army for its use, or sold them. He could have returned them to Darius, making an extremely magnanimous gesture that we would wonder at even today. He could have had them killed immediately. He could have ransomed them. What did he do? He retained them, befriended them, and allowed them to retain their royal status. Eventually, he became a close friend to Sisygambis (Darius's mother). Later he married Darius's oldest daughter Barsine (subsequently renamed Stateira after her mother), which further helped cement Alexander's identity as the Persian king.

Inferences and Allegations

Why was this action a virtuoso deed? Was it because the queen was an exceptional hostage? Was it because with such a hostage he gained leverage over Darius? Or did Alexander just see himself as a hero, who was required to treat Sisygambis with magnanimity? Whatever the motive or rationale, this incident has come down to us as one of the most significant stories about Alexander.

Leading Lessons

Today, when we acquire a company, we may demand outward conformity to our culture, norms, and policies, though perhaps not inward commitment. However, it is the inward commitment that will make the greatest difference in the long run. So, how can we engender that commitment? If a firm is repeatedly fair and even magnanimous to employees of acquired firms, the firm is more likely to acquire commitment. Future employees who are acquired with their company will get honest information that they too will be treated fairly. Fairness will make them more cooperative both during due diligence (you will get much more accurate data) and after the merger. Perhaps this was why Alexander befriended Sisygambis.

A modern example of the rewards of gaining commitment is how banks, during periods of rapid acquisition following deregulation, handled the reconciliation of the different policies (e.g., pay scales, benefits, job titles, and so on) of each institution. When the reconciliation was handled to the benefit of all employees, they subsequently became zealots for their employers, which helped to improve a bank's customer service. When very highly paid specialists were acquired, though, they were handled like the extraordinary human resources they were, and they were allowed to keep their privileged pay scale and other benefits. The lesson? Treat royal hostages well.

On the other hand, when is the concept that Alexander practiced in Turkey—"pillage, burn, destroy, and send the news ahead"—more effective? (See Chapter 4.) Both concepts will change the reality to which you subsequently respond—enacting the world. However, applying the correct approach requires artistry. In the beginning, with limited resources, Alexander had no choice. By later in the campaign, he faced options, and magnanimity became one of those options. Pillaging does not create alliances, though it can reframe a problem. In the beginning, magnanimity would not have worked to reframe or solve the problem.

14: On Marriage and Leading in a Multicultural World

By late in the Persian campaign, Alexander had to address how to integrate diverse peoples. The Greek soldiers were especially resistant, apparently seeing this crusade strictly as one of conquest, not sharing any of Alexander's nobler ideals. Alexander, however, adopted the clothing, customs, and manners of other cultures. He also married into other cultures. Once he was the de jure king of the Persian Empire, he took the building of alliances among the various peoples of the domain and the Greeks and Persians very seriously.

When Alexander visited Bactria and captured the hilltop fortress called the Rock of Sogdiana, he captured the nobleman Oxyartes, whose daughter was an exceptional beauty named Roxane. Rather than merely taking her as war booty, Alexander married her, and it is said he fell in love with her. (Incidentally, during their entire marriage, they never spoke the same language.) She was the only *wife* to bear him a male child or heir and so assumed quite some importance in the Bactrian scheme of things. While this union endeared him to the locals, it alienated the Macedonians because Roxane was considered a barbarian. That would imply that Alexander's son, should he live to inherit, would himself be half barbarian.

A mass wedding between as many as 10,000 Macedonians and Asian or Persian women at Susa in 324 B.C. marked the beginning of the serious integration of the two cultures—Greek and Persian. Already Alexander had incorporated Persian ministers, governors, generals, and soldiers into his administration; married a Bactrian princess; permitted existing governors to continue in office; paid dowries when his soldiers married locals; paid all of his soldiers' debts; and personally adopted Persian garb and some Persian customs. Though still married to Roxane, he now married two more women: Stateira, who was the oldest daughter of Darius III—the king he had recently deposed and whose death marked the end of the Achaemenid dynasty—and another Persian woman.

Alexander strongly encouraged a policy of multiracial fusion. However, the common soldiers strongly disapproved. Their racism was the beginning of yet another revolt. They did not want a mixed race of administrators and generals, nor apparently did the Macedonian leaders, if we take as evidence that after Alexander's death only one Greek nobleman remained married to a Persian woman. The straw that broke the mutinous camel's back was the arrival of 30,000 Macedonian-trained and outfitted Persian soldiers, who joined the core of the army. This was such an affront to the Macedonians that they "revolted" at Opis. Alexander responded by attempting to placate them with the offer that wounded veterans, as well as those who had served their allotted time, were free to return to Greece. However, this offer backfired because the troops were insulted and assumed that Alexander meant to replace them and dismiss their loyalty and service. Mutinous leaders emerged and threatened to take the entire Greek army home. Alexander was "incandescent with rage," took to his tent, and then started appointing Persians to the officer

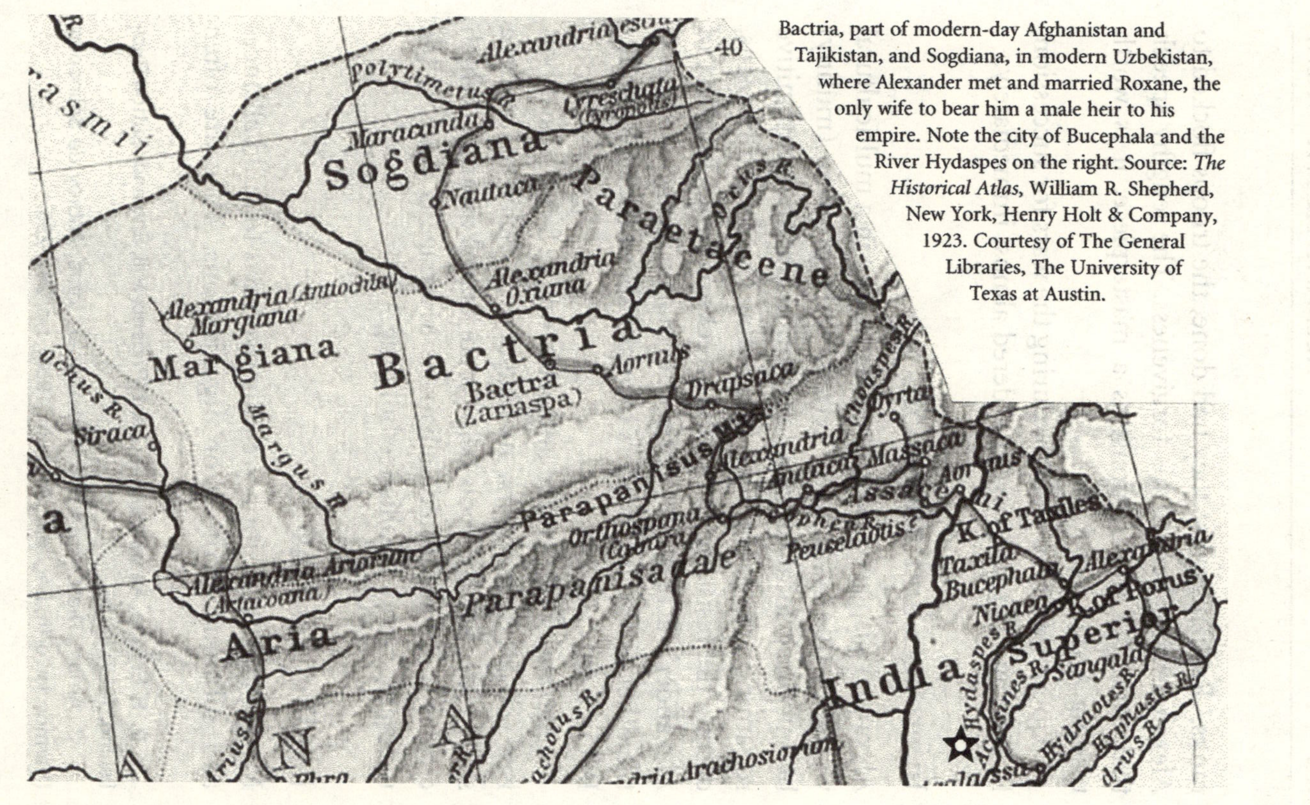

Bactria, part of modern-day Afghanistan and Tajikistan, and Sogdiana, in modern Uzbekistan, where Alexander met and married Roxane, the only wife to bear him a male heir to his empire. Note the city of Bucephala and the River Hydaspes on the right. Source: *The Historical Atlas*, William R. Shepherd, New York, Henry Holt & Company, 1923. Courtesy of The General Libraries, The University of Texas at Austin.

ranks.[2] Realizing what they had done, the troops flocked to Alexander and begged his forgiveness. The lengthy speech that extracted this response is a masterpiece; it is worth reading Arrian just for it.[3]

Upon Alexander's death, during the wars for succession, Roxane and her son were murdered almost immediately.

Inferences and Allegations

Alexander displayed exemplary leadership in a multicultural world. In this example, he reframed the problem (mutiny) by imposing local officers (an administrative, nonpunitive reframing). He got his way, integrating Greeks and Persians, despite the resistance of all the Greek soldiers. The effect of Alexander's action was as though Martin Luther King and the other civil rights leaders brought about the Civil Rights Bill in a day.

Alexander recognized and acted on the fact that symbolism (of dress, manners, marriage, etc.) helps to create a shared identity. Symbols help create shared meaning, which creates unity and builds alliances. Marriage is possibly the ultimate symbol of alliance building.

Leading Lessons

Merger and acquisition are only two ways to build alliances and subsume territory or organizations. They are often

2. E. E. Rice, *Alexander the Great* (Phoenix Mill, England: Sutton Publishing, 1997), p. 86.

3. Arrian, *The Campaigns of Alexander*, trans. Aubrey de Sélincourt (Harmondsworth, England: Penguin, 1958), pp. 292–295.

transitory—replaced by better deals. If a subsidiary of the target acquisition does not fit the business model of the new entity, it is sold off.

Other forms of alliance, like marriage, can be more enduring. Indeed, this may be the way to guarantee survival. Marriage is a *symbol* of alliance building, and symbols may be a key to alliances, not the merger itself. For example, when America Online (AOL) and Time Warner merged, they were nearly equals. Just a few years later, when the promise of AOL seemed empty, it was dropped from the corporate name and became just another subsidiary of Time Warner. Contrast this example with having a Starbucks in every Barnes & Noble store. This is a symbolic union—not a marriage or merger.

Integration is essential. The reality is that our world is multicultural and will become more so. There will also be those who resist integration, thinking of themselves as conquerors. Replacing "Macedonians" with "Persians" will go a long way toward appearances of integration, but it does not win over the hearts of racists. That is, you may get outward conformity, but not inner commitment. Leadership can make the difference, and each situation is different. Threats are potent. Actions are more potent.

When two insurance companies merged, the corporate headquarters were consolidated and power was shared. One firm's CEO took the helm of the merged entity, and the other took the job of president. Upon the CEO's retirement, the president took over and dozens of top managers were swept from office, or else they left for their own reasons. The pendulum swung back a decade later when one of the first CEO's protégés took over. Finally, the drastically different cultures commingled. Integration of cultures in corporate America can easily take more than a decade.

We saw Alexander's offer of early retirement backfire, initially. This tells us the obvious: In mergers, consider how various strategies will be treated before you act. Anticipate responses contrary to that which you wish to happen.

15: Battle at Gaugamela

How, you might ask, can destroying an army build alliances? The Greek and Persian cultures could not be merged while a Persian army could be fielded. Sometimes you have to destroy to build.

After winning battles at Granicus and Issus, conquering Tyre, and then wintering in Egypt, Alexander swept east toward the Persian heartland—modern-day Iran and Iraq. By the spring of 331 B.C., Darius had assembled a formidable army, whose size is variously misreported for propaganda by ancient authors. It is universally acknowledged that it was much larger than the Greek army because, upon engagement, the Persian flank extended well beyond Alexander's.

Upon arriving at the artificially leveled field of battle, Alexander's soldiers confronted an army that was fatigued from having stood to all night. The battle was met with an oblique line, in order to give the smaller Greek army an opportunity to create and exploit a breech in the line, which is exactly what Alexander did. He and his Companions (his elite cavalrymen) personally chased Darius from the field (a story made famous by the image on the mosaic tile floor at Pompeii), causing a general rout even among the much larger Persian army. The chase after the rout continued well into the night. (Reports of casualties vary, at one extreme reporting a loss of 500 soldiers for Alexander but 100,000 for Darius, which further supports the extreme disparity in size between the two armies.) Darius escaped, but he was later murdered by his own generals, as we will see in Chapter 3, Lesson 25, "Death of Darius III." The army captured most of Darius's personal belongings at the town of Arbela.

Inferences and Allegations

Never again did the Persians field an army against Alexander after Gaugamela. So humiliating was the defeat that the Persians never again regrouped. The fate of Darius, which is traced to Alexander's relentless pursuit of him and those who fled with him, was the demise of the Achaemenid dynasty.

Leading Lessons

I am not one to blithely advise mass firing to ensure culture change. However, sometimes deconstruction is the only way to begin a merger. Always finish the job. A wounded and humiliated workforce is a dangerous workforce—eliminate the division or integrate it into your organization, but do not leave the job half done. When resistors cannot be won over to the new culture, you must eliminate them or find a way to work around them. For example, General Motors (GM) encountered extreme resistance from its unions because of decades of poor relations. The unions could not be "fired," so GM set up a new division, Saturn, which enabled it to establish new work rules, a new culture, and a new competitive line of cars.

The idea of building alliances by deconstruction occurs not just at the level of organizations. At the level of an entire economy, governments sometimes have to act with a heavy hand. John D. Rockefeller's tactics at Standard Oil were so perfect at eliminating competition and creating a monopoly that when federal legislators wanted to draft antimonopoly laws, they just examined Rockefeller's organization and strategy and used them to guide the laws that made most of those activities illegal. To make the U.S. economy a fair playing field for all, it was imperative to destroy organizations that impeded fair competition. Today America, indeed much of the world, has "free" markets unimpeded by trade barriers, antitrust laws, and limitations on cooperative ventures such as cartels. The resultant set of alliances has created wealth worldwide on a scale never heretofore imagined.

Concluding Thoughts on Building Alliances

Alexander was a military genius. We typically picture military leaders who are renowned for their battlefield acumen. But Alexander will be remembered at least as much for his empire-building skills. He built teams, governments, and peoples. His alliance-building insights are unmatched in history.

Alexander enlarged a defeated king's territory after defeating him (earning Porus's loyalty after the Battle at the River Hydaspes); befriended his enemy's mother, wife, and daughter (after the Battle at Issus, and later marrying the daughter); married someone who did not speak the same language (the Bactrian princess Roxane, who bore him his only legitimate male heir); prepared to let a "barbarian" inherit the kingship (Roxane's son by Alexander); and chased a king from the battlefield to initiate a new dynasty (the much reproduced mosaic at Pompeii shows this scene at the Battle of Gaugamela). Such a wide range of alliances illustrates an important leadership lesson.

A submariner once pointed out to me that despite my obsession with Alexander the Great, alliances and cooperation are far more important in strategic planning and implementation than are battles and other forms of competition. Alliances with suppliers, distributors, manufacturers' representatives, customers, trade groups, government regulators, standards organizations, and other such entities make the difference between success and excelling. When I finally realized how critical alliance building was to Alexander, I affirmed the submariner's assertion and recognized it as a central tenet of enactment. The question becomes this: When do we use the carrot instead of the stick, pleasure instead of pain, and magnanimity instead of terror? However you answer that question, alliances change the world to which you subsequently respond, and they create a world easier to lead.

Alliances occur on all levels. We can build an alliance with individuals: employee-employer; wife-husband; protégé-disciple; consultant-client; salesperson–purchasing agent; flight attendant–passenger; teacher-student; editor-author. We can build an alliance with an organization: preferred supplier, long-term purchasing contract, reciprocal marketing, cobranding, foundation challenge grant, insurance provider. Or we can build alliances with greater entities: a company committing to stay in a community in exchange for tax advantages; state authorities building transportation between adjacent states; treaties between countries; military alliances; trade agreements; schools and universities preferentially providing graduates to companies in exchange for money, products, scholarships, or other services.

In every case, if we create an alliance, we change the world in which we move. The alliance may be a short-term change, or it may be for life.

CHAPTER 3

Leadership Process Three: Establishing Identity

Identity is a critical process by which members of organizations arrive at a shared understanding and attach a shared meaning to their activities. Many scholars have demonstrated that identity is a socially constructed phenomenon. The process of forming an identity creates unity where it was lacking before. Identity can be built by an individual (e.g., adults develop as we acquire more experience) or among individuals (e.g., turning strangers into a coherent unity), cities (e.g., turning enemies into a league), or peoples (e.g., creating an empire). As will be shown, Alexander often manipulated the development of identity among his own troops and even among his conquered subjects.

This process transpires on at least two levels, and they are intermingled. First, we all create our personal identity, starting in childhood. This chapter, and earlier ones in this book, deal with who Alexander was or was becoming. Second, as leaders, we establish our organization's (or political unit's) identity. The intermingling is when the two processes occur together. Organizational, cultural, and country identities are examined in the latter part of this chapter.

16: Succession

Who was Alexander? Who would he become? Would he have a kingship from which to begin his career? Much of what Alexander wanted in life seemed to depend first upon his succession as king of Macedonia.

Philip's "primary" wife, Olympias, sired Alexander. However, Philip did have eight wives and many legitimate and illegitimate children. Despite the number of siblings, Alexander was raised to believe he was to be the heir to his father's kingdom. For example, he was a key lieutenant in Philip's army, and he was educated (by Aristotle, among others) to be king.

On the occasion of Philip's final marriage, to a woman named Cleopatra (also called Eurydice), Alexander overheard Eurydice's uncle, a general of Philip's, invoke a divine blessing that this union would result in a legitimate heir. Not yet twenty, Alexander exploded in a blind fury, causing his father to draw a sword against him. Only extreme drunkenness on Philip's part saved Alexander's life. After the event, Alexander and Olympias were exiled from the court. The succession was thrown into doubt. After Philip's murder, Alexander and Olympias fought all for Alexander to win the throne.

In Macedonia, internecine struggles were the norm. Upon his return from exile, Alexander ordered all royal contenders to the throne, including his cousin, killed (or he killed them himself). Olympias almost certainly eliminated the last wife (Cleopatra, whose uncle had provoked the exile) and her infant daughter. Olympias remained in Greece during the subsequent campaign and helped hold the alliance together, almost ruling on Alexander's behalf, maintaining a loyal vigilance.

After his father's death, Alexander confirmed the appropriateness of his ascendancy by pursuing Philip's policies. First, he convened the League of Corinth, convincing them to elect him as his father's successor (as hegemon). He next quelled revolts in the north (in Trace, Illyria, and on the Danube) and returned to deal with a revolt in Thebes.

Inferences and Allegations

In this case, given the fundamental importance of being king, Alexander bided his time. He was patient when others might have acted expeditiously or inappropriately. When the opportunity did arise, he acted decisively and immediately.

Leading Lessons

So many organizations lack sound succession plans at all levels of the organization. Lack of an agreed-upon succession plan can lead to chaos. Succession is often not smooth and requires structural change to accommodate different management styles. Without sound plans, those that ascend to the top leadership position often wreck havoc with others in top management, to the detriment of the firm.

Another lesson is that sometimes we have to bide our

time. Political forces can put or retain our personal competitors in positions that block our inevitable ascendancy. This is common in politics and all kinds of organizations. It is an important lesson for us all.

17: On Killing Your Childhood Friend

Who we are changes dramatically over time. Good leaders keep these changes well monitored, if not under control. As our identity changes, so must our outward manifestations of it, our body language, and our communication style.

Alexander had completed the conquest of Persia, became king upon Darius's death, and was now subduing the various eastern tribes that plagued Persia and refused to acknowledge Persia's primacy.

In Samarkand, Alexander was enjoying a drinking bout, a common occurrence, at a religious banquet. Understand that Alexander did not drink water; rather, wine was his all-day, everyday beverage. This was common, but most people diluted their wine with water (thus "purifying" the water). By not cutting his wine, Alexander essentially lived his life intoxicated. A drinking bout would have involved an even more substantial intake, and probably substantial inebriation. During this banquet, flatterers were comparing Alexander and his accomplishments to various gods, and one sycophant asserted that Alexander had surpassed his own father, Philip II. Cleitus, a childhood friend who had even saved Alexander's life at Granicus, was apparently tired of Alexander's Persian ways and the flattery. In a drunken state, Cleitus launched into a tirade against him. Alexander did not take it well and attacked his friend. Others attempted to restrain him. However, the tirade continued and Alexander furiously struck Cleitus down with a spear through his heart, killing him.

One report says that Alexander was so grief-stricken that he immediately attempted to kill himself. Others said that he took to his tent and refused food for a week. Whatever the response, he killed his good friend while under the influence.

Inferences and Allegations

There is no excuse and no justification that can lessen the demonic nature of this beast. It seems that as Alexander got older, he needed *more* reassurance of his greatness, despite his unparalleled accomplishments. This need perhaps suggests a lesser greatness, but one that can be learned from. The leadership literature does point out that adversity helps to develop great leaders. Without intending to trivialize the incident, he *is* called Alexander the Great, *not* Alexander the Perfect.

Leading Lessons

Different writers and different readers could conclude some serious and not-so-serious lessons: Beware sycophants; impetuousness rarely turns out well; some actions are irreversible; do not drink to excess; and try to keep from putting a spear in your friend's chest.

However, as an educator of thousands of leaders and a coach of CEOs, executive directors, managing partners, and every other titled leader, I believe that a universal lesson is to know yourself. People think they do, but people change so rapidly that their knowledge, even of themselves, is rarely real-time. For example, burying a parent, sibling, spouse, or child changes us. We all know immature adults who are obliviously still working out some issues from earlier times and may never finish. Many good leaders have a definite blind spot about themselves; just ask their spouse, children, or peers.

It is nearly impossible to cite a modern, specific example that is not trivial, because the real afflatus is private, not public. However, Lance Armstrong survived testicular cancer and went on to win the Tour de France five times. FDR was plagued with polio. Ulysses S. Grant was an alcoholic. Great leaders often carry their demons around inside them. Almost all successful leaders have had their own adversities that define them (at least for a while).

One of my greatest challenges as an educator is to show that sense of self is not the same as self-knowledge. Learning who we are and who we want to be are two of the most difficult tasks of a leader (sense of self). Manslaughter doubtless redefined Alexander to himself and his compatriots. Knowing yourself intimately is vital to preventing such tragedy. Learning from similar tragedies is painful, but necessary.

18: On Heroes

Whom we admire, openly, speaks volumes about us. It helps establish our identity (i.e., who we are). The actions we take to substantiate our regard for those heroes also reveal a bundle about us. Contrast the heroes of someone who collects sports memorabilia with the heroes of someone who collects rare antique maps.

Alexander desired to start his campaign as auspiciously as possible. He made appropriate sacrifices everywhere he went in order to create the appearance that he wasn't a conqueror but a liberator, and wasn't a threat to the locals.

When Alexander crossed into Asia, near the site of ancient Troy, he did several things in recognition of his heroes from Homer. For example, he was the first to leap ashore and throw his spear into the ground, which signified that it was "spear won" land. He is said to have paid obeisance to the tombs of all the Trojan War heroes, especially Achilles, Ajax, and Priam. He even went to the trouble of visiting the Temple of Athena in Troy for further dedications. In particular, he took from the temple a set of armor from the time of the Trojan War and had it symbolically carried before him when he went into battle, all the better to make clear who he was and whom he emulated and revered.

All of the extant classical sources refer to Alexander's near reverence for Homer. Plutarch even relates that Alexander slept with a copy of the *Iliad* under his pillow. We do not know if this is a veridical assertion, but that we even discuss it today buttresses Alexander's identity.

Inferences and Allegations

Imagine you set out to exceed all the accomplishments of the greatest people to precede you. Whom would you look to for guidance? Alexander recognized, even late in his life, that he constantly had to aspire to even greater greatness.

Leading Lessons

Everyone needs a hero. Even heroic figures such as Alexander. Alexander's hero was Homer and the heroes he wrote about. Alexander was hero to Caesar, Augustus, Napoleon, Frederick the Great, Louis the XIV (the Sun King), and untold others.

Who are your heroes? Why are you reading this book but to aspire to greatness? The fact that you go to the trouble of reading it suggests that you choose great heroes. Let others know who your heroes are and why. I am convinced that one of the most important skills of a leader is storytelling. Stories relate compelling lessons. Not only can you influence people with your choice of story, but you'll influence the perceptions people have about you by your choice of leader and story. Let others know who your heroes are; it may help to establish your claim to greatness, or at least help win succession tournaments.

19: On Life and Death

How we die says something about who we were. Alexander was a general who truly cared for his troops. It is said he knew the names of 10,000 of them. He was regularly observed treating his soldiers' wounds himself, before he permitted his own wounds to be tended to. He shared their hardships on the march. His last act, while deathly ill, was to personally say good-bye to each member of his army. One might say his army was his identity.

Alexander died in Babylon at age thirty-three, having covered more than 10,000 miles in just over ten years, conquering the greatest empire the world has ever known, integrating diverse peoples, introducing coinage, revolutionizing trade and commerce, and promulgating a common language and culture, among other accomplishments.

Shortly after his closest friend, Hephaestion, died at Ecbatana, Alexander himself grew ill with fever. Toward the end, his army asked to see him and filed by. For each soldier, he raised his head and signaled acknowledgment with his eyes.

Despite vulgate records and endless speculation, we do not know for sure what caused Alexander's death. It was fairly sudden, possibly preceded by copious drinking (which was nothing new for Alexander). During the fever, he repeatedly bathed in the river. He ate little. Some speculate that he was not dead but rather just in a coma, because his body did not putrefy for weeks. He probably died of a tropical disease.

An impossibly grand funeral was held, but most important, a funeral bier was built that, according to Arrian, was so large, composed of so much gold, and so grand, that it became an immediate tourist attraction. The bier was to be brought back to Pella, but was expropriated by Ptolemy (one of the Companions, a childhood friend of Alexander's, and a rumored half-brother), who took it to Alexandria in Egypt and founded a dynasty there. Every tourist, from Roman emperors to slaves, visited the bier for centuries. Nero probably stole it for the gold to be melted down. Alexander's body disappeared without a trace. In the late twentieth century, a Greek archaeologist found evidence of Greek writings in Siwah. The archaeologist contends it may well be where Alexander's body was interred.

Inferences and Allegations

Alexander was mortal, despite being considered a god in his lifetime. The funeral bier would have helped consolidate his identity and his successors, and it would have strengthened unity by being displayed throughout the empire on its return to Pella. Irony is a jealous god—it turned out that Alexander's body, once it was stolen by Ptolemy, actually contributed to the empire's disintegrating immediately after his death.

Leading Lessons

In the end, we are all mortal. Buddha put it better than anyone: "We have all been dying since we were born." Recognizing this fact while we are alive may extend or improve the time that endures. Whether anything can be made of your death probably depends upon your will and the reliability of its executor. What is the real, enduring legacy we will leave behind: a gilded bier, cities, knowledge, a reputation, an army, or a unified civilization?

I suppose this whole book is about asking the questions, "Who are you?" and "What do you want out of your life?"

20: Reverence for Predecessors

Paying homage, affiliating yourself with esteemed predecessors, restoring revered places, sincerely quoting others' speeches, copying cherished attire, mannerisms, or symbols—all these actions can potently amplify your reputation, prominence, and identity.

By the time that Alexander had thrice defeated the Persians in major battles, Darius III was now on the run. Alexander paused in his chase to attend to a symbolic matter that helped to further his and his Persian identities.

Pasargadae had been the royal city of the Achaemenid dynasty for as long as anyone could speculate. When Alexander visited it, he found that the grave of Cyrus the Great had been desecrated. He authorized, indeed commanded, that the tomb be restored.

We can only infer what was going on in Alexander's mind, but several guesses are not bad. First, he could have simply been respecting royal prerogative. His handling of both Darius's body and Porus's reinstatement (see Chapter 2 on the aftermath of the battle at the River Hydaspes) support this contention, though this is unlikely given his treatment of others. Second, in anticipating his own demise, Alexander may have been preparing the way for his own posterity—the extreme irony of his own body's abduction notwithstanding. Third, he could be further ingratiating himself with the Persians to help maintain his own legitimacy.

Inferences and Allegations

Alexander, while an alcoholic, a killer of friends, a paranoid, and a slaughterer of innocents, had a magnanimous streak about him that served him and his history well. By attending to *all* royal households, he furthered his own legitimacy and identity.

Leading Lessons

Leaders know not to ridicule, blame, mock, or censure their predecessors. You may part company with their policies, strategy, vision, and culture, but you do so without directly criticizing the previous administration. However, the additional lesson here is that by revering predecessors, especially worthy ones, you take away some of their eminence—perceptual theft by association, if you will. All Roman emperors found opportunities to associate themselves with various predecessors. Modern leaders commonly emulate Alexander.

21: On Transportation

In modern times people obsess about what car they drive. Wise leaders know that the only obsession is not what others think, but what we think of ourselves; that is, who we are. Outward accoutrements leverage what others believe.

Even as a child, Alexander asserted himself memorably. His father acquired a horse that no one could ride, and he offered it to Alexander, if the boy could mount it.

Alexander tamed this enormous black horse that even his father could not calm to mount. When Alexander succeeded, his father gave him the horse as a gift, and it remained with him throughout his campaigns, dying in Central Asia. He named it Bucephala. The horse allowed Alexander always to ride first into battle, always to be visible, and always to be first among his Companions, the elite Greek noble cavalrymen. When Bucephala died, he was given a substantial funeral and a city was founded on the spot.

Inferences and Allegations

Alexander succeeded as a very young man, almost a boy, where others, even adults, had failed. Taming and riding a great beast helped to forge Alexander's image and identity at a young age. What does that mean for us? If we haven't succeeded by late childhood, we never will? No, of course not.

Leading Lessons

What might possibly be the modern equivalent of a great "untamable" steed? A beautiful car, a boat, office furnishings, a house, a spouse? The closest parallel we have today is purchasing an expensive car, though it is not remotely as powerful in identity building as Bucephala. Symbols help promote identity. But one person's symbol is another's identity. Wise leaders use symbols only to manipulate others' perceptions to their own advantage. This could mean driving a humbler car to work and saving the exotic car for private consumption.

We all know people who drive exotic cars and can afford them. However, this often, ironically, lessens our perceptions of them. They are just ostentatiously showing off their wealth. We also all have friends who drive a nicer car than they can afford, because they really love driving a fine car, but they cannot afford it and have to give up other luxuries. Our image of such people is enhanced.

22: Sycophancy or Obeisance?

How shall we be known? How shall we be called? How shall we expect our subordinates to address us? What appearances shall we portray to the world? Most important, how we answer these questions will determine who we are or are known to be.

By the time the conquest of the Persian Empire was complete, Alexander was indisputably the greatest king in the known world. He sought outward recognition of this fact.

Proskynesis was the traditional form of obeisance offered as a matter of course to the Achaemenid king. The details are not well known, but the greetings of veneration ranged from a slight bow for high-level nobles to abject genuflection for peasants.

Alexander instituted proskynesis, though the Macedonians strongly resisted. To them, it was humiliating—their king was ostensibly an elected equal. One cannot be certain, but it would have made sense to maintain this practice for the local populace, given their accommodation to it; but to the Greeks, it was just one more example of Alexander's becoming too self-elevated. This transgression of propriety (setting himself up as a god) lowered the Greeks to the level of the "barbaric" Persians.

Inferences and Allegations

Alexander sought to unify cultures, countries, armies, and governments. He apparently thought that traditional symbols, gestures, and actions, while insulting to his own countrymen, were essential to governing a foreign land whose citizens expected such displays. He used a simple symbolic act to create an identity—though it ran counter to the battlefield identity known to his own soldiers.

Leading Lessons

Consider protocol carefully. It can have an important purpose, but too little or too much can be harmful. In modern organizations, there exist so many forms, symbols, artifacts, and expressions of obeisance that leaders need to think quite carefully about adopting any equivalents of proskynesis. Some executives have a corporate helicopter, or an aircraft fleet, or an array of apartments, limousines, butlers, and suites. You could only conclude they are significant kings. They use these appurtenances of office because they can, without ever thinking about whether they should, given the symbolic expressions of their use. Perhaps the example of one of my mentors will suffice. Upon taking over as CEO, he eliminated all chauffeur-driven cars, all box seats at sporting events, all memberships at golf and eating clubs, and by executive fiat, dropped millions of dollars to the bottom line of a multibillion-dollar concern. It cost a small diminishment to the egos of leaders who should have known better in a regulated industry under siege.

23: A Lack of Vision

A vision bounds or unbounds an organization. The vision creates the identity of an organization. A plan helps to achieve that vision. Once he was Persian king, Alexander had to determine the reach of the empire. What would Persia be under Alexander?

With the Persian kingship his, Alexander set off for the east to secure or expand the empire's borders. With the murder of Darius, Alexander faced a substantial decision that would affect all the rest of his life, and the fate of the empire. Persia had for a long time loosely laid claim to large tracts of what was incorrectly referred to as "India"—modern-day Afghanistan, Pakistan, and adjacent regions. Never had clear, uncontested control been established in these regions. We know that Alexander consolidated his control in the heartland by appointing various Greek and Persian satraps to the multitudinous positions throughout the empire. But why he ventured east is pure speculation. It is completely unclear to current historians what Alexander's intentions were. Did he intend personally to subdue all the various hill tribes? Nothing survives that reveals Alexander's thinking or intent—all is inference.

Whatever the inference, it occupied him for six years. He received numerous wounds; conquered numerous towns, cities, fortresses, and peoples; founded quite a few cities; buried his great horse Bucephala (where he also founded a city); fought one great battle (at the River Hydaspes); crossed the Gedrosian Desert; and eventually returned to Babylon to die young.

These years were a relative wasteland, given the greatness of his early accomplishments.

Inferences and Allegations

Alexander could be cited for consolidating the empire he inherited—creating a more identifiable whole than the vagueness that preceded him. That alone would warrant greatness. Also, Alexander's curiosity, shaped by Aristotle, was insatiable, so he may actually have intended eventually to subdue China.

Leading Lessons

Why Alexander expended so much time is inexplicable, and I will not try my hand at meager speculation. However, I will ask the reader to introspect, merely by observing the obvious—that all of us have periods in our lives that are less productive than others, that we often make decisions whose implications we have to live with for years, decades, or even the rest of our lives. Even the greatest of leaders have their bad periods. These periods of stupidity and doubt may produce enduringly bad decisions that haunt them. We shouldn't abuse ourselves too mercilessly. Introspect and learn from those failings, and they are not wasted. Mistakes are usually our most important teacher.

On a more positive note, we should all be reminded that every organization needs a strategic plan. Without one, we often find ourselves adrift, chasing ephemeral goals but forgetting our larger purpose. Vision and plans remind us and our organizations of our larger purpose.

24: Alexander's Letter to Darius

When promising young leaders attain seemingly outrageous accomplishments, especially with limited resources, one wonders who they are. Letting the world know who you are is critical. Even more important is how you let the world know.

After the battle at Issus, Darius wrote a diplomatic letter to Alexander, king to king, asking for the return of his family and household goods. The response was a masterpiece of reality and identity creation.

Darius III—the reigning Achaemenid king of a thousand-year dynasty to whom other kings paid homage, the penultimate ruler of the known world—had to have wondered who this young upstart was. Who was this man who seemed to have accidentally defeated Darius's armies twice? According to the vulgate sources (which, while not completely reliable, have foundations in reality), Darius sent a letter, the response to which by Alexander follows:[1]

> Your ancestors invaded Macedonia and Greece and caused havoc in our country, though we had done nothing to provoke them. As supreme commander of all Greece, I invaded Asia because I wished to punish Persia for this act—an act which must be laid wholly to your charge. You sent aid to the people of Perinthus in their rebellion against my father; Ochus sent an army into Thrace, which was a part of our dominions; my father

1. Arrian, *The Campaigns of Alexander,* trans. Aubrey de Sélincourt (Harmondsworth, England: Penguin, 1958).

was killed by assassins whom, as you openly boasted in your letters, you yourselves hired to commit the crime; having murdered Arses with Bagoas' help, you unjustly and illegally seized the throne, thereby committing a crime against your country; you sent the Greeks false information about me in the hope of making them my enemies; you attempted to supply the Greeks with money—which only the Lacedaemonians were willing to accept; your agents corrupted my friends and tried to wreck the peace, which I had established in Greece—then it was that I took the field against you; but it was you who began the quarrel. First I defeated in battle your generals and satraps; now I have defeated yourself and the army you led. By god's help I am master of your country, and I have made myself responsible for the survivors of your army who fled to me for refuge: far from being detained by force, they are serving of their own free will under my command.

Come to me, therefore, as you would come to the lord of the continent of Asia. Should you fear to suffer any indignity at my hands, then send some of your friends and I will give them the proper guarantees. Come, then, and ask me for your mother, your wife, and your children and anything else you please; for you shall have them, and whatever besides you can persuade me to give you.

And in future let any communication you wish to make with me be addressed to the King of all Asia. Do not write to me as to an equal. Everything you possess is now mine; so, if you should want anything, let me know in the proper terms, or I shall take steps to deal with you as a criminal. If, on the other hand, you wish to dispute your throne, stand and fight for it and do not run away. Wherever you may hide yourself, be sure I shall seek you out.

Inferences and Allegations

Here we see genius. Alexander was a shrewd politician and a practical businessman, always with an eye on his immortal reputation.

Alexander redefined the situation in Asia by a single document. First, Alexander is the king of Asia, not Darius. Second, Darius is the criminal, not Alexander. Third, Alexander is magnanimous. He could have treated his prisoners several different ways (see Lesson 13, "Royal Hostages," in Chapter 2).

Leading Lessons

First of all, leaders must be clear and assertive—even audacious. Learn to create your own reality. The preponderance of reality is retrospective. Since the victor writes the history, bring your own historians, as Alexander did. Most "autobiographical" CEOs do. Surviving documents tell the only story. You control the story to an important extent by your writings. Write. Write with an eye on history.

The heart of the Persian Empire—modern-day Iran. Alexander fought a major battle at Gaugamela. Ecbatana was summer capitol of the Achaemenid kings. Persepolis was the Persian capitol. Susa, a major city and treasury under Darius, was the site of the mass wedding of Greeks and Persians cited in the text. Source: *The Historical Atlas*, William R. Shepherd, New York, Henry Holt & Company, 1923. Courtesy of The General Libraries, The University of Texas at Austin.

25: The Death of Darius

Despite having defeated his satraps once (at Granicus) and Darius twice (at Issus and Gaugamela), Alexander still could not claim to be king. Darius had to be killed. Only this death would establish Alexander's identity as king.

After the palace at Persepolis was burned, Alexander continued the pursuit of Darius to Ecbatana, a wooden hill fortress used by the Persian kings as a cooler summer retreat. The army had just missed Darius at Ecbatana, so Alexander departed with just the cavalry to chase him down. The foot soldiers would follow more ponderously.

There is little agreement on exact events, though the outline of what transpired follows. The consensus is that Darius was dead before Alexander's cavalry caught up with the fleeing, dispirited remnants of the army. Alexander had Darius's body returned to the royal capital (the burned Persepolis) for a proper funeral.

The more interesting, if slightly less credible, account is that Darius's ministers and generals recognized how precarious their position was, if captured, and agreed to kill Darius, send his head to Alexander, and plead for clemency or at least mercy. The rumor that survived in the vulgate sources is that a eunuch boy named Besius, who had been one of Darius's favorite lovers, was dispatched with the head in a silk bag to plead for the Persian ministers' lives and fortunes. It is quite certain that this very beautiful boy became Alexander's lover also.[2] Alexander absorbed the

2. Mary Renault explores this story and views of the two royal households in her wonderful book *The Persian Boy* (New York: Bantam, 1972).

Persian elite into his own government and army, which initiated some of the growing hostility toward him for becoming too inculcated in the Persian culture.

One might wonder what this says about loyalty.

Inferences and Allegations

Alexander immediately made managing his new domains much easier by sparing and acquiring the possible loyalty of the old ministers. This made the difference between acquisition (conquest) and merger (generously sparing their lives).

Leading Lessons

Accept the fealty of sincere lieutenants. Becoming king requires authority. Once you take the position (whether through a death, coup d'état, mass movement, or usurpation), read Machiavelli: "Men will pledge their lives and their fortunes until called upon to do so." Careful selection of your predecessor's lieutenants can rapidly help you secure your new position, though it also burdens you with their baggage. Becoming the head leader requires careful management of the accoutrements, appurtenances, and privileges of office; of former officers, managers, and leaders; of the two or more cultures and the other contenders who require special attention. Conversely, do not get stuck with incompetent predecessors who make leading convenient for you, because you will lose the zealotry of others.

Concluding Thoughts on Establishing Identity

There is almost no leadership process more powerful than establishing identity. Who we are, as an individual, a team, an organization, a society, and a people, is paramount. An individual breaks the four-minute mile, a team creates a breakthrough product, an organization creates a political party that changes the world, and a seemingly insignificant people can humble superpower military machines. Too many leaders today seem to grossly underestimate the power of identity.

Reconsider the examples from Alexander's brief life:

- Eliminate rivals (including family, to secure the throne).
- Know yourself upon adversity (killing Cleitis accidentally).
- Have heroes (Homer).
- Secure a good executor for your will (control events after death; Alexander's body was kidnapped by Ptolemy to establish legitimacy).
- Pay homage to your predecessors (tend to others' good names).
- Tame the horse (it wouldn't hurt to get attention very young).
- Require genuflection, if appropriate (don't demand too much protocol).
- Integrate the workforce and keep your vision clear (you can't pursue your vision after your death, but your zealots can).

- Write and change reality (your letters create reality).
- Accept the fealty of sincere lieutenants (after the murder of Darius, Alexander fused the Greek and Persian administrative apparati).

If we revisit the levels of identity building, individual and organizational, we see universal applications to all leaders today. First, let's look at the individual perspective. It is commonplace for leaders to assume that they must try to find themselves, or to know who they are. Yes, these are important activities. But at least equally important, yet harder to teach and much harder to do, is to consider and become who you *want* to be. The difference is looking inside and trying to be who you really are, then looking outside and deciding who you *will* become. Inside, outside. Past, future. Were, will be. I suppose you need to be true to yourself, but we all change so much that it is an equal supposition that you let go of who you were and become who you can be. There may be an Alexander the Great inside all of us, but we suppress that heroic inside figure.

I began this book by pointing out that "leadership cannot be taught; it can be learned." If you are to grow as a leader, *you* must do the learning. My experience is that only experience—on-the-job experience—can teach leadership. Some of us are better at learning from experience and others are slower. The adage that wise people are just people who have made more mistakes than you is an adage worth remembering. Leaders make mistakes. That is how they learn. The best leaders are those who permit lower-level leaders to learn from their mistakes. I believe that organizations must forgive honest, well-intentioned mistakes. How else can organizations develop their next generation of leaders? Alexander made horrible mistakes. Most of us have too, though maybe not killing a close friend. What we learn from that mistake is what makes us better. If we dwell on it and allow the past to immobilize us, we do not grow and become tentative in the future. If we think about it, learn from it, and move on, we grow.

The second level of identity building is organizational. Simply put, the primary job of a leader is to create organizational reality by promulgating a vision, creating or overseeing the creation of a plan, putting together a team, and helping that team implement that plan. Each activity changes the world in which we operate. Vision gives the organizational members a new target and a new identity. A plan (developed with the team) advises us how to achieve that new reality. The team does the work, making the leader the chief human resources officer and head identity builder. Monitoring the team's implementation helps us achieve what we conceived.

When he died prematurely, Alexander was building one identity out of two primary cultures that were incompatible. Identity building today seems to me to be underappreciated and not pursued as vigilantly as leaders should. I recently had the privilege of observing Marine Corps officer selection and training for four days in Quantico, Virginia. I was flabbergasted, literally, by the careful selection and training processes in place for recruitment, selection, and development. There is nothing in industry that even remotely comes close to the identity building that is central to the Marine Corps. No wonder their culture is so powerful and enduring. Civilians have much to learn from the likes of Alexander and the Marines. We must learn to better integrate and manage our cultures and our organizational identities. Symbolism, our next enactment process, is a robust tool in identity building.

CHAPTER 4

Leadership Process Four: Directing Symbols

There is robust literature that investigates when and how people attribute actions to leaders, even when the attribution is inappropriate. A leader can direct the use of symbols and thus influence followers' attributions, due in large part to the salience of the leadership role and the cognitive response elicited by symbols. Symbols are also important because through them a leader can create sustained meaning, shared interpretation, and joint action. Controlling symbols is a source of power for leaders. This power is akin to that of a movie director using another's script, but causing the story to unfold in such a way as to retain the director's prerogative for shaping the final outcome.

Using symbols and the cognitive attribution assigned to these symbols was critical to Alexander, who viewed symbols as part of tactics. By blurring the distinction between the environment and the organization, and between problem and solution, Alexander reframed problems and used symbolism to alter the environment.

26: Utter Destruction

Sometimes reframing a problem is done using symbolism. The representation of a symbolic act can be far more compelling than the act itself.

At the very start of the invasion of Asia Minor, but after the battle at Granicus, Alexander faced the task of conquering dozens of small and a few large hilltop citadels with very limited resources.

On the western coast of modern-day Turkey, Alexander confronted an impossible situation. He had only a small army, but he confronted a formidable number of small cities, towns, citadels, and fortresses. He clearly could defeat any one of them, or even several. But each pursued siege would further reduce his army due to death, injury, and additional needs for garrison duty. Alexander needed to find a way to get the towns to capitulate without a fight and without requiring him to garrison every town.

Alexander sent out diplomats to let all towns know that he wanted them to overthrow their Persian overlords. Some joined him; some wanted to, but the Persians held family members as hostages; and others were content with the Persian presence. His solution to this recalcitrance is considered today to be reprehensible (although there are modern-day equivalents after hostile takeovers). His purpose was to make such a lurid symbolic statement that subsequent towns would not dare impede his progress; indeed, they would capitulate without resistance. To do so, he made a horrible example of one town, whose name today is unknown because court historians were ordered not to record the name, thus making the erasure of the town complete. The recalcitrant town was besieged and conquered. While the captive citizens watched, Alexander's army looted the town. They tore down the city walls, burned the buildings, and salted the fields so no one could grow crops there in the future. The women were then systematically raped while their men watched. Then, all the men and male children were killed while the women watched. The women, female children, and maybe some young boys were then sold into slavery, except for a few, who were sent down the coast ahead of the army to tell other denizens what had transpired.

Needless to say, any city without a sizable Persian garrison capitulated without a fight. Who in their right mind would resist, facing such a fate? Thus, Alexander was able to conquer an entire region fighting only one such skirmish. While he did have to besiege one large city (Halicarnassus), starve another into submission by blocking its harbor (Ephesus), and subdue a rebellion (Miletus), he was able to continue his incursion without much hindrance.

Inferences and Allegations

Alexander redefined the reality of thousands of people in dozens of towns by the horrific symbolic action of utterly destroying a town and its people. As horrible as this destruction is, it caused countless peoples to side with him, without his having to fight them. He clearly showed the seriousness of his purpose. He showed that he was capable of anything. Tyrants throughout history have effectively used such knowledge to their advantage. It enabled him to conserve scarce human resources at the cost of the innocent. You may prefer this example be put in a chapter called "Lesser Great Acts." It is less great, but the logic is unimpeachable.

Leading Lessons

We can (and historians do) quibble and debate about the horror of the one town and whether such behavior was "appropriate" to the times, but such debates are beside the point for our learning from Alexander. Does history remember Alexander as a mass murderer or a victorious general?

This lesson is extremely difficult to convert to modern times. Although Alexander's action demonstrates how you can successfully manipulate human nature, if he were a general today, he would be court-martialed for such action. An executive today using similar civilian actions would be under scrutiny for illegal or unethical behavior. Having said that, sometimes legal and ethical behaviors that get things done are not nice behaviors and today would be avoided by most—but not all—executives. A classic example is that of Robert Moses, who was responsible for reshaping New York City and the surrounding boroughs so thoroughly over the course of decades. Moses resorted to blackmail, physical threats, intimidation, and other "hardball" tactics. In some circles, Moses is considered a monster, and the heaping of abuse upon him and his reputation is warranted. In other circles, people admit that while his techniques (like Alexander's) were heavy-handed, he got things done that almost certainly would *not* have been accomplished otherwise. This may be Machiavellianism, where the ends justify the means, but this is also prudent, careful, thought-out use of power, symbolically enhanced to reduce subsequent resource expenditures. Applied with rarity, toned-down modern versions of extreme actions may be justifiable.

27: Illness at Tarsus

Our actions can build (or destroy) trust. By coupling our actions with symbols, we enhance that trust; we enhance the effect of the action compound ways.

In the second year of his campaign, before the second great battle (at Issus), Alexander paused at Tarsus and fell gravely ill with cramps and fever—in fact, all his physicians but one feared that he could not recover. Unfortunately, the only physician who did *not* despair, Philip of Acarnania, was the very one about whom Alexander had received a letter asserting that he intended to poison him. Furthermore, Philip proposed to treat Alexander with a powerful (read risky) admixture of drugs. Against the strong advice of his colleagues, Alexander agreed to the treatment. At the very moment Alexander began to drink the potion, he handed the accusing letter to the physician. The rumor was untrue. Alexander recovered. Philip was magnanimously rewarded.

Inferences and Allegations

The symbolism of quaffing a possibly poisonous potion while the rumored assassin is reading the assertion is one of the most delicious images in humankind's history. Alexander was an enigma about trust. He believed in people until they taught him not to, but at other times he was paranoid. Much later in the campaign, he also became more paranoid about trusting his father's advisers. How do you reconcile such schizophrenic behavior?

Leading Lessons

The lesson? Trust people. Rumors can be very destructive and must be stopped ASAP. If you are trusting of your people, you can be a more effective vehicle of change. Getting people to trust you is the key. Using symbolism can convert trust into zealotry toward your mission.

A wonderful story from World War I about saving face helps to further support and explain Alexander's action at Tarsus. It also illustrates how great leaders symbolically acquire trust. Two promising and highly regarded captains had never met, but they happened to be commanding adjacent units on the front. They walked out in front of their troops, saluted, shook hands, removed their helmets, and began a conversation. Coincidentally, the Germans began a walking artillery barrage, which crept closer and closer to them. Rather than one of the captains losing face and suggesting the prudent expedient of putting on their helmets and retiring to their trenches, both stood there having their conversation while artillery fire rained down around them. Luckily, they were not hit. Their names were Patton and MacArthur. They went on to become two of the most important generals of World War II, acquiring exaggerated reputations for courage under fire. Courage of your convictions is imperative. Demonstrating those convictions is equally important. Symbolism enhances them. In other words, trusting your physician is one thing; drinking a possibly poisonous potion while accusing the physician while you do so is quite another symbolic thing altogether.

28: Reign of Terror

Symbolism can keep far-flung administrators in line, but only if you make an example of one or a few. How enduring the amalgamation will be depends on how visible the symbolism is.

Near the end of his life, after surviving the debacle in the Gedrosian Desert, described in this chapter, Alexander began the long march back to Babylon. As he passed through the various administrative units, he discovered that many of the satraps whom he had appointed had usurped their territories and presumptuously taken royal powers, behaving as though they were kings, not Alexander's administrators.

Alexander's appointed satraps obviously presumed that they would never see him again. This presumption cost numerous governors their lives, and yielded serious punishments for most others. This revealed that the administrative structure of the empire was fragile at best. There is no evidence that Alexander corrected the process of administering this huge realm, and the empire disintegrated shortly after his death. However, he made examples of the presumptuous and acted swiftly.

Inferences and Allegations

Alexander recreated reality. He redefined the problem from how to administer lands to how to keep "decentralized" administrators in line—a common problem in all organizations today. The symbolism is that the leader *could* return. Should a leader return, punishment will be swift and severe.

Leading Lessons

Readers of this book have probably made the same mistake early in their leadership careers. You may have failed to adequately clarify your role in a new position, and then overstepped that role while earnestly trying to achieve the best for the organization—but discovered too late that the boss disagreed with your boundaries. Some of us are lucky enough to have bosses who understand that this is a leadership lesson learned on the job. Others have bosses who are autocratic terrorists and do not permit learning. Make sure when you assume a leadership role that you understand the boundaries of your position. Alexander symbolically made clear the permissible latitude of his governors: Rule in *my* stead, not yours.

29: Leading from the Front

It was said that for breakfast, Alexander liked a long march and for dinner, a light breakfast. Leading requires showing the way. It requires that you do not ask others to do what you yourself would not do. If you lead the way by putting yourself in jeopardy, you can achieve near mythological proportions.

Alexander was profligately careless with his own life, and this example, very late in the campaign, simply exudes leadership by example.

After the battle at the River Hydaspes, the army proceeded down the Indus to battle the Mallians. At their strongest citadel, Alexander, who always led from the front, engaged in his most foolhardy act, nearly costing him his life. While on the wall, he jumped down into the city to avoid being shot by arrows, but there he encountered severe, nearly rabid attacks. A few Macedonians were able to reach him, but not until he was severely wounded. He was carried, near death, to the camp. So wild with anger was the army over the presumed death of Alexander that the city was reduced and all inhabitants—women and children included—were killed. This was the height of the army's butchery.

The army sorely feared for Alexander's life—rightfully so because his demise would probably have led to the dissolution of his army. He did recover, despite his extensive loss of blood, and the army reveled in his recovery.

Inferences and Allegations

Alexander led by example, in all circumstances. His example was commendable in that the more dire the situation, the more likely he was to be in the fray.

Leading Lessons

Lead from the front, but don't be foolhardy about it. If you take stock options, see that all who contribute to the bottom line also get stock options. If the union is taking a pay reduction, so too should you. If productivity is an important initiative, be visibly more productive. If you reduce the number of dancers in your ballet, cut administrative staff, at least symbolically. In the Marine Corps Officer Training Program, officers are taught that soldiers come first, *not* the officer. After a tough march, the soldiers are fed and sheltered before the officers.

30: Cutting the Gordian Knot

Today the phrase "cut the Gordian knot" is a cliché, implying "make it happen" or "get things done." How did it become one? Alexander cut the Gordian knot. But what most people do not know is that the task was to *untie* the knot. This impossible task was handled symbolically. Visiting the knot was brilliant, but untying it was a lie. Perception is more important than reality when symbols are involved.

After subduing the coast of modern-day Turkey, Alexander spent nearly a year—one could say he wasted a year—traveling through the central portion of the country. The most noteworthy event was his encounter with the Gordian knot.

For centuries there existed the myth of this complex knot, made of a special bark, which united the yoke and tongue of an ox cart. In the West, we are commonly knowledgeable about the Arthurian tradition of Excalibur: "He who pulleth this sword from this stone shall rule England." In antiquity, "he who could untie the Gordian knot would rule Asia" (which for all intents meant the whole world). Alexander may have pursued the Gordian knot to sanction his inevitability, support his claim to heroism, bolster his ego, enhance his visibility, embolden his army and generals, impress the locals, embellish his reputation, intimidate Darius, or maybe all of these reasons and more that we can scarcely guess. Whatever the reason, the outcome was perfect public relations.

Historians are not at all clear on what happened. (It is

important to stress that in this case historians really do not know the facts. I am speculating based strictly upon more modern re-creations of the knot and common sense.) The knot *was* undone. The question is whether it was untied or cut. One version of the story is that Alexander figured out how to pull a pin out of the midst of the knot and undo it. But modern reproductions of the knot show that the way it is tied, it *cannot* be untied. (The bark is folded under itself while wet, and when it dries, it is impossible to move it at all, let alone manipulate it to untie it.) Therefore, the second version—wherein Alexander got frustrated, drew his sword, and cut the Gordian knot—is the more likely version. Regardless of what happened, his PR machine let it be known that Alexander had untied the knot.

Incidentally, that night there was thunder and lightning. Alexander's entourage felt that this activity supported the belief that he had fulfilled the legacy of the knot. Note that the truth is irrelevant. All that matters is what the entourage, and, subsequently, history, felt was true.

Inferences and Allegations

Alexander created a new symbolic reality, one that sanctioned his invasion and conquest. The expediency of using his public relations machine to convey what he wanted to be true was all that was required.

Leading Lessons

It is tempting to place tongue in cheek and assert that sometimes it takes a sword to cut through bureaucratic inertia.

However, there is a more important lesson to conclude. Perception *is* or *becomes* reality. It is in our power to leverage perception through the use of shrewd public relations, advertising, and report writing. For example, in what is one of the most honest advertisements ever placed, General Motors admitted in full-page ads that its cars had been the best thirty years ago, that they were terrible for decades, but that they have dramatically improved in quality and are now on a par with the world's best. Perhaps this is an exaggeration, but it is nonetheless a very powerful assertion that will doubtless have an effect on perception (sales will follow) exactly because of its honesty.

Sometimes reality isn't good enough. We may embellish our accomplishments, be it a résumé, our performance appraisal, our annual report, or our earnings. It is wrong to do so, and embellishment is not the lesson to take away. The lesson from Alexander is not to lie; but if there is a symbolic opportunity, take it. I *am* trying to show how symbolism can influence perceptions. In other words, you need to identify what symbolic act will gain buy-in from your followers. Find a way to complete that act, even if it is not exactly as prescribed. People will appreciate the symbolism and the effort. They will *want* to believe. For example, organizations that seek to win awards are using symbols to amplify the public's perception of their accomplishments; other organizations tirelessly execute in quiet obscurity—same performance, very different perception.

31: Battle at Granicus

Early in the campaign to invade Persia, everything Alexander did would have significance beyond the mere event. Probably with his eye on history, he played to both the Greeks and history.

At the very beginning of the invasion, Alexander encountered the army of the local satraps who foolishly, it turns out in hindsight, did not burn the crops ahead of him, but rather sought to defeat Alexander in battle. He also faced Greek mercenaries hired by the Persians.

In 334 B.C. Alexander crossed the Hellespont with an army probably comprised of 30,000 to 40,000 infantrymen and 4,000 to 5,000 cavalrymen. The first of Alexander's four major battles was fought at the River Granicus against the local satraps and their local contingents, who were soundly defeated, despite having a superior tactical (i.e., geographic) position behind a small river. The particulars of this battle are in slight dispute. Some say the battle was joined in the late afternoon, coming on the heels of a ten-mile march. But others, whose narrative makes more common sense, suggest that Alexander waited until dawn for a surprise attack on the army, which was camped a mile or two behind the river. When finally engaged, Alexander's adversaries badly organized their troops with the cavalry (i.e., nobility) in front. In either case, reports agree that Alexander bravely led from the front, had his horse wounded under him, and met with the wounded afterward to encourage them to brag of their exploits and explain their wounds.

There is also disagreement about the aftermath of the battle. It is known that the dead, both enemy nobility and Greek mercenaries, were buried. But the fate of the 15,000 Greek mercenaries captured alive is unclear. One account had them mercilessly slaughtered, a huge symbolic atrocity designed to dissuade any other Greeks from entering the service of the Persians against the Macedonians. However, it is probable that these 15,000 were returned in fetters as slaves to Macedonia to face a lifetime of heavy labor—which would have a similar, though more productive, effect on any Greek considering mercenary service against Alexander.

After the battle, Alexander shipped to the Athenian acropolis 300 sets of Persian armor, as a symbolic dedication from Alexander and the Greeks. This symbolic gesture honored Athens. The accompanying inscription to be carved in stone pointedly excluded mention of Sparta, which had just as pointedly not joined the League of Corinth.

Inferences and Allegations

Alexander displayed three great symbolic attributes. First, he endeared himself to his soldiers after the battle. Second, he provided important public relations for the civilians at home. Third, and most important, his treatment of the Greek mercenaries (possible slaughter, probable enslavement) sent an unequivocal signal to potential mercenaries.

Leading Lessons

This battle and its aftermath suggest two related lessons for employee and public relations. Assuming you lead from the front (modeling the way), you gain the ability to relate on special terms with employees. As a general example, a dean without teaching experience has a different relationship with the faculty from someone who has shared extensively in a core business of a university. A specific example is that of Disney's CEO Michael Eisner, who insisted that top managers spend at least a week a year at the theme parks so they could better understand and personally experience what the employees face, how the theme parks fit into the integrated business model of Disney, and how guests are treated. The idea is to understand the business by staying close to the core.

Pay attention to the media, and manipulate them to your advantage. Alexander's sending the Persian armor back to Athens was a persuasive, undeniable, and compelling symbol—a gesture rooted in Greek symbolism. Ever since the Trojan War of the *Iliad,* armor had great symbolic value. Here the statement is one to the troops of their success, as well as one to the Greeks of Alexander's worthiness to lead them. Notice that "public" gestures are made often as much for the employees as for the audience. A modern example is Stew Leonard's rules for his grocery store chain, which are proudly and visibly displayed on a large boulder right in front of the entrance at corporate headquarters: Rule 1: The customer is always right. Rule 2: When the customer is not right, see Rule 1. This is clearly for public consumption and for employees and customers. The symbolism of a gigantic boulder representing the very basis of the business is delicious.

32: Sleeping Before the Battle at Issus

Appearances can immobilize an army. Rumors can arrest bravery. Fear can halt hope. Alexander was exceptional at engineering symbols to change appearances, undo rumors, and render hope.

The second of the four great battles that Alexander fought was at Issus. The two armies had passed each other and cut off each other's communications. Darius passed to the north, intercepted some ambulances, and massacred the men. This news enraged the Greeks, needless to say. At that time, Alexander was south along the coast.

Alexander's army was outnumbered, and his generals were deeply concerned, a concern that spread to the troops. The geographical setting was the tactical solution to the concern. The exact location of the battlefield is unknown, but even today it is clear that this plain is hemmed in on the east by mountains and to the west by the Mediterranean, which greatly restricted the ability of the numerically superior Persians to deploy. Alexander slept past dawn, the symbolism of which was not lost on the troubled generals. By showing an arrogant disregard for the overwhelming size of the opposition, Alexander broadcast unequivocal disdain for the Persians, which helped quell his subordinates' fears.

During the battle, Alexander broke through the center at a critical moment, chased Darius from the field, and caused the Persian army to break, rout, and run.

Inferences and Allegations

Apparently no one but Alexander realized that army size did not matter given the geographical disposition of the battlefield. By sleeping late, he promulgated disdain for his opponents, which charged his army with hope, courage, and victory.

Leading Lessons

Once Alexander realized that the terrain favored him, he conveyed his confidence to generals and troops alike by the simple symbolic expedient of sleeping soundly. This implies that you should think about your problems but not worry about them. This is an important distinction. Worry unproductively causes you to lose sleep. Thought enables you to solve problems.

Apple Computer was an indescribably insignificant underdog in the beginning, yet the company has bedeviled IBM from its inception. The company selected a market segment that was absent IBM and consistently carved it out for Apple. When IBM finally responded, its top leaders realized that IBM culture was so pervasive, and so counter to what would be required of a desktop computer team, that IBM senior management needed to take several symbolic steps to distance the new IBM PC team from the old mainframe computer company. For example, they organizationally set up another strategic business unit. They physically located the new company unit in a very laid-back place (Boca Raton), and the PC team members abandoned the famed IBM "uniform" (blue suit and white shirt) for extremely casual wear.

In entering a job market when the economy is down, most aspiring applicants panic, worry, and passively wait. A thoughtful applicant accepts the situation and creates such powerful symbols that an employment offer is inevitable. For example, do your research; find a sponsor in the organization; know the employees of the target company; know the target company's business better than any applicant; call unknown people by name; propose bottom-line solutions unconsidered by employees; etc. Knowing more about the company is a symbolic and extremely compelling action. When you impress line leaders enough, they will hire you.

33: Ablutions, Celebrations, and Other Correct Behavior

The leadership literature is addressing celebrations more and more. The significance of attending symbolically to whatever accomplishments or matters warrant attention is underappreciated by many leaders.

During his campaigns, Alexander traveled through an impossibly diverse geographical, religious, and cultural landscape. Upon entering Babylon, he was greeted as a liberator. He immediately ordered the restoration of temples that had been destroyed by the Persians after Babylon rebelled more than a hundred years before. The jubilant Chaldeans (priests) were indebted to Alexander, and through them, the people welcomed Alexander as one of their own.

Everywhere Alexander traveled, he held sacrifices, games, and festivals to placate the gods at the local temples. The effect, of course, was to ingratiate him with the locals. He sought to find parallels between his gods, sacrifices, and divinations and the local gods so as to portray himself as a pantheist who was accepting of the local "heresy." This was a pattern that was repeated throughout his life—he always performed the correct ablutions, sacrifices, festivals, games, or whatever was locally correct.

Inferences and Allegations

Alexander recognized the symbolism of local-minded people. Never assuming his sacrifices and ablutions to be "correct" and never doubting his own beliefs, he played the perfect pantheist—religiously placating everyone everywhere he went.

Leading Lessons

Confusion about gender, religious, and cultural differences requires acceptance, understanding, sensitivity, and broad knowledge. Sometimes leading requires the finesse of a pantheistic "priest."

Mergers and acquisitions warrant careful regard for local gods, customs, and celebrations. For example, when Unilever acquired Ben & Jerry's Homemade ice cream company, it was extremely careful to pay close attention to all the things that made Ben & Jerry's unique. Unilever continued the practice of environmental awareness—to an obsessive degree. It continued the extraordinary orientation toward the employees. It changed few human resource policies, even though they were considered anathema in most of the rest of the capitalist world. Furthermore, Unilever made good public relations out of its fidelity to the original culture at Ben & Jerry's. This attention to detail helped convey the important reality that Ben & Jerry's is unlike any other organization in the world.

34: Crossing the Gedrosian Desert

Alexander's symbolic action in the Gedrosian Desert not only saved his army from dehydration, but it ranks as one of humankind's most noteworthy symbolic gestures.

Toward the end of the campaign, after the "mutiny" in India, Alexander set out to take a different route home to Babylon, by way of unknown territory—hoping to fill in geographical knowledge conspicuously absent from existing maps.

In September 325 B.C., Alexander started his march through southern Gedrosia. This region included one of the planet's most inhospitable deserts. Alexander's intention was to sustain the fleet if needed by digging wells along the coast, but mostly for the fleet to deliver water to the army as needed. Unfortunately, his reconnaissance yielded bad information. (Local guides purposely misled him, hoping the army would perish in the desert.) He was unable to provision the fleet or receive water himself because the coastal region had sheer cliffs that prohibited access to his ships. Alexander and his army ran out of water. People started dying.

Having shared so much hardship over the course of the campaign, the army had become so loyal to Alexander that they pooled their remaining water (literally squeezing the last drops out of their goat-bladder canteens) to offer their king. The water was presented to Alexander in a large silver helmet at an assembly of all. The troops knew that they were all going to die, but they could provide enough water for their leader to live. Think of the sacrifice being made by thousands of disciplined soldiers!

Alexander realized that he would lose this magnificent military machine if he didn't do something. But how do you save an army that is dying of thirst without benefit of water?

Alexander poured that helmet full of water into the sand in front of the assembled army. He spoke to them with a clear message, "I will share your fate." Before Alexander poured the water out, the army's fate was to die, but Alexander was to live because of their generosity. After pouring out the water, Alexander, too, would die. Alternatively, the army could walk out of that desert with Alexander to assure that the fate he shared would be to live. So they did. Now, it is only fair to mention that noncombatants suffered terribly, and many, many people died. But it is the consensus of modern medical doctors that no one should have walked out of that desert.

Inferences and Allegations

Alexander redefined the army's reality through one simple symbolic gesture and a few well-chosen words—changing fate from "going to die" to "have to live." Why can't you?

Leading Lessons

To fully understand the impact of what Alexander did, it is useful to relay an incident that occurred more than 2,000 years later. During World War II, Britain was so strapped for sailors that the merchant marine fleet needed to rely primarily on those who were not called to active military duty. This meant that the fleet was manned by older men, from fifty-five to seventy years old, and boys, some reportedly as young as fifteen or sixteen. Well, of course, the German submarine fleet sank dreadful numbers of merchant ships, especially early in the war. Many sailors survived the torpedoing of the ships by escaping into lifeboats. Some were picked up immediately, but many languished for up to weeks in the open sea with very little food or fresh water. The obvious expectation was that the older men would die of exposure and the young men (boys, really) would survive. After all, the young men were in the physical prime of their lives, and the older men were, put politely, past their prime.

Exactly the opposite occurred. The young men tended to succumb and the older ones lived. Why? Well, the man who would later found Outward Bound investigated this phenomenon after the war and discovered a pattern. For example, one who voluntarily deprives oneself of food may live twice as long as one who is forced to be without food. Similarly, you can choose to go without water for several days, but if you are deprived of it, you die more quickly. The older men survived because they had reasons to live—a garden to finish, a wife to see to, and grandchildren to help raise—whereas the younger men had less encouraging them to return. Strong wills became more crucial than strong bodies. It was this principle that inspired the establishment of Outward Bound. Yet, more than two millennia earlier, Alexander led his troops out of the desert with this same principle.

Perception *is* the cognitive battle. Symbols are an essential tool to manipulating perception. Symbols can win a battle. Symbols are a leader's most important perceptual implement. With them, you can change the world.

Of course, you carefully consider the symbols you use consciously. But are you aware of the symbols you use inadvertently? I once dealt with a small family business where the management team sat in carpeted and air-conditioned splendor while the hourly people sweltered on the shop floor without so much as a fan for ventilation. Any attempts to ask the union to make concessions in such a symbolically charged atmosphere were doomed.

Gandhi used symbols more effectively than almost any leader of modern times. For example, he led the Salt March, gathering followers along the route as he trekked day after day, arriving with an audience of many thousands. He then took ocean water, boiled it, put the residue salt in a paper envelope, and sold it at auction. At the completion of the transaction, he and the highest bidder were arrested by British authorities and jailed for violating the British monopoly on the manufacture and sale of salt. This event, a symbolic affair of the utmost impact, initiated the failed attempt to occupy nonviolently the Dharasana Salt Works. The attempt resulted in hundreds of pacifist Indians being beaten by armed guards, while the "besiegers" did not raise a hand. It was the end of Europe's moral suasion in India. The expulsion of the British was won symbolically.

Concluding Thoughts on Directing Symbols

Leaders are in the business of influencing perceptions: those of employees, direct reports, superiors, the board of directors, stakeholders, stockholders, communities, the media, the customer, the union, and everyone else. The most powerful way to create a new perception is through careful application of symbols. Most of the time we use our everyday symbols without even thinking about them. But the best leaders understand the role of symbols in enacting realities different from what everybody else believes.

Alexander provides a plethora of ideas about the capabilities of symbols:

- Utter destruction can convey a new power (obliteration of hilltop town in Turkey).
- Trust people, sometimes (drinking poison at Tarsus).
- Keep administrators on track (dealing with disloyal executives upon return from the East).
- Lead from the front, i.e., set the example (everywhere; all the time).
- Cut the knot (use of public relations after cutting the Gordian knot).
- Send captured armor home and return mercenaries in fetters to slavery (let symbolic acts not be lost on your home base).
- Sleep soundly (think; don't worry).
- Placate local gods symbolically (attend to appropriate local beliefs).
- Use symbols to manipulate perception (i.e., pour out the water).

So underappreciated is the power of symbols that leaders who adopt their appropriate use will find themselves outmaneuvering all others. It is empirically well established that observers inappropriately attribute action to incumbents in roles. For example, *The New York Times* asserted on its front page that "Reagan Revises Tax Code." That is patently untrue. In reality, hundreds of people labored for over a decade, led by a few key senators and members of Congress and their key staff, who had no idea which party would be in office when they completed their task. Therefore, they wrote a relatively politically neutral revision of the tax code. To give the credit for this action to Reagan is a travesty. However, President Reagan was brilliant at manipulating the symbols of office and took full advantage of—and credit for—the revision. Since observers make inappropriate attributions, leaders can systematically influence observers' perceptions. And there is no better way to so influence than by the use of symbols. Contrast the use of heat and air conditioning in the White House. Nixon liked the rooms colder in summer so he could enjoy a fire in the fireplace. Carter put on a sweater and turned the thermostat cooler in winter, in front of millions of television viewers, to plead with Americans to use less imported oil during the embargo. Carter's application was impeccable.

We all know coworkers who strut around taking credit for others' work, showing off how wonderful they are, and generally clogging communication channels, especially vocally at meetings, to imply how indispensable they are. Such people are usually unmasked for what they are. I plead that you learn how to use symbolism, but not to overuse it.

CHAPTER 5

Concluding Thoughts About Leadership

Leading is an art. There is some science behind it, but artistry makes the difference between a good leader and a great leader. Your curiosity has taken you on a quest involving a leadership artist—Alexander the Great. You have learned many lessons from this reading, and you will apply some with panache, some with finesse, but some execrably. As an artist, you will not give up, but learn from your mistakes.

I contend that this process approach to leadership has power. I have offered four processes that help make that power accessible to practitioners like you. Let us review the processes and get a better perspective on their application now that we've completed the historical journey.

1. *Reframing problems is a cognitive tool that can change the world.* For example, our foreign policy is dictated to a significant extent by the dependence of the U.S. economy on foreign oil. In the aftermath of 9/11, a president would

almost certainly have had the support of the civilian population to make the sacrifices necessary to reframe the problem. Currently it is a problem of finding, pumping, transporting, and processing crude oil, all the while securing every step, no matter where in the world. A president could reframe the issue as a domestic problem: higher fuel efficiency, local production, conservation, and a faster conversion to a hydrogen economy, all in the name of patriotism, which would sell well in America. Just think of the symbolic opportunities to embellish the reframing.

A Taiwanese business builds inexpensive patio furniture and sells it to all of the low-priced outlet stores, such as Kmart and Wal-Mart. Almost all manufacturers are in Taiwan with production facilities near Shanghai, on the mainland. It is essentially impossible to gain a cost advantage in this circumstance. Profit margins are low, products are nearly interchangeable, and increasing market share is problematic. The sales cycle is annual, with trade shows in the United States being where the primary contracts are made for the coming year. One business executive in Taiwan reframed the problem to the excruciating detriment of all the competitors. This one man vertically integrated backward into pigments—he bought a supplier. It turns out that more than 80 percent of all low-end steel patio furniture is white. The pigment supplier was the monopsony supplier in China of that white pigment. Once he owned the pigment source, he ceased selling it to his competitors at the critical moment, when it was too late to acquire supply elsewhere. His firm ended up getting a huge leap in U.S. business, because, of course, it was able to fill orders and the extra demand, too. Now, this activity may not be nice. But this reframing of a problem changed the world of patio furniture manufacturers to the advantage of this one leader. Reframing and problem displacement (acquiring the supplier) worked.

2. *Building alliances is a common tool in a leader's tool kit.* Alliances can become octopuses that work for you, creating a new world in which to do business. For example, I stumbled into a nexus of businesses that were extensively interconnected. A law firm handled the needs of a major bank and, of course, that bank handled the banking needs of the firm, and most of the senior partners. Okay. Senior partners from the firm moved into senior management positions at that bank and sometimes later returned to their partnership at the law firm. Okay, again. The law firm also handled the legal needs of a large insurance company, which happened to provide for the insurance needs of both the bank and the law firm, with both services reciprocated. Not too surprising. Well, coincidentally, one accounting firm audited the books of these three firms. Guess what? The law firm handled the auditing firm's legal needs. A local university had relationships with all these firms, and all these firms actively recruited at the university. Hmm. Every organization provided its services to every other organization. There are numerous other intricate interconnections, such as board memberships, that we need not investigate. You get the picture. Everything is perfectly legal; nothing diminishes competition; and indeed, all the firms were better off. In this situation, alliances were carefully built by

leaders at all the organizations, resulting in strong benefits for all. Learn and use the power of building alliances.

3. *Establishing identity is paramount to leadership.* My experience with top leaders is that they pay inadequate attention to culture and organizational identity. The evidence is clear: Organizations with a strong culture outperform those without one. I ask rhetorically, "In how many organizations is culture an afterthought?" Organizations that systematically build the identity of their employees excel. This is true whether you are building cars, making symphonic music, or invading countries. Identity matters to people. The adage is that we all want to belong to something larger than ourselves. This sense of belonging makes the difference between two stonemasons, one who reports "I cut stone for a living" and the other who asserts "I am building a cathedral." Same job, very different commitment. Establish and build identity in the workplace.

The other aspect of identity is self-identity. This topic warrants its own book. Who you are and who you become are essential to being a great leader. Both are open to enactment. You can act to change who you are and who you will become by using all four leadership processes.

4. *Directing symbols, the final leadership process, is probably the least consciously used and most misunderstood process.* Let me again assert the caveat: Do not become a symbolic manager by abusing the power of symbols. Everyone will see through you and isolate you, making you ineffective. However, learn to use symbolism effectively, which probably implies rarely. Symbols are all around us all the

time: our clothing, our haircut, our cars, our office, our desk, but most commonly and importantly, our words. External symbols can help strengthen our words. Together they can change our organizations, our industry, the supply chain, the customer, or even the economy.

Symbols are interesting also because they can be used in the other three leadership processes. For example, Alexander used the symbolism of pouring water to reframe the situation of his army dying of dehydration in the desert. He married the former king's oldest daughter to form an alliance. He rode a huge black horse and wore an ostentatious helmet and plume so his troops could see him leading from the front, which established one part of his identity. In general, you must pay attention to the symbolic fallout of existing symbols and then learn to anticipate how to use them for effect.

At the conclusion of World War II, General Douglas MacArthur was to receive the unconditional surrender of senior Japanese military and political leaders. His overriding problem was how to guarantee that the war was really over, that renegade Japanese elements would not continue guerrilla warfare on the four main islands of Japan.

The Japanese considered Americans to be little more than barbarians. They held almost all foreigners in contempt. Such an attitude would not make administering postwar Japan easy. MacArthur had to figure out how to transform this disdain into respect. (Incidentally, historians after the conclusion of the war discovered that most Japanese leaders felt that Americans did not understand the Japanese and that only MacArthur did. He was their greatest fear. This fear could be used to MacArthur's advantage.)

He chose to accept the surrender on board the battleship *Missouri* in Tokyo harbor. Furthermore, he insisted that his senior officers not wear weapons. His advisers strongly fought this, pointing out that one single renegade Japanese officer could kill MacArthur and other senior leaders. However, MacArthur knew that by not having weapons, symbolically showing American superiority and fearlessness would have an enormous effect on the Japanese. He was right. The Japanese were deeply impressed. This is how MacArthur began to reframe the Japanese problem.

He argued Japan should be America's greatest ally in the Pacific Rim, and he set about developing a constitution (he wrote the entire first draft himself) that would recreate Japan as a democracy, having powers incumbent in the populace that could counter the natural militaristic tendencies of the samurai trading houses that dominated the post-Meiji era and eased Japan into World War II. So, his constitution gave universal suffrage to women, who had been extremely marginalized before. He legalized labor unions. He created a two-house parliament with a prime minister on the British model. And he ruled the postwar nation with a magnanimity bordering on zealotry. America's enduring relations with Japan are attributable to MacArthur.

Directing symbols, building alliances, establishing identity, and reframing problems. Brilliant.

CHAPTER 6

Concluding Thoughts About Alexander

I first learned of Alexander the Great, other than through awful college textbooks, when I was stuck in an uncharacteristic summer rainstorm in the Greek Isles in the early 1980s. I ran out of reading material and stumbled upon a used copy of Arrian, which I read at first out of desperation, and then with a growing sense of wonder. I had recently finished three graduate degrees from an Ivy League university and was learning more about leadership and strategy reading this one book than in all my years of higher education. I marveled at the deficiency of our educational system, and vowed in my own way to change it. This book is my fulfillment of that vow. I cannot do Alexander justice, but rather take a high-level overview of some of the greatest lessons and leave the details to you for a lifetime homework assignment.

Who was this man? He certainly had impressive titles: King of Macedonia, Pharaoh of Egypt, King of Kings. He founded numerous cities, some of which still flourish. He brought the very idea of a Greek-style king to Asia, where three successor kingdoms continued to employ it and expand it after his death. He revolutionized trade by introducing coins and establishing a common language for long-distance commerce. Indeed, trade flourished across an entire continent where mostly local barter existed before. Greek culture, religion, and art spread throughout enormous expanses where it had heretofore been unknown. Military architecture had to be changed because of the need to be able to resist the siege towers that Alexander introduced to Asia. One could go on and on. Tarn put it succinctly when he asserted that "he was one of the supreme fertilising forces of history. He lifted the civilized world out of one groove and set it in another; he started a new epoch; nothing could again be as it had been."[1] I believe that is not overstatement.

I end with an apology. He came to be known as Alexander the Great, not Alexander the Perfect or Saint Alexander. He did horrible things to people, he made terrible mistakes, but he changed the world irredeemably. Despite his shortcomings, I offer three larger-than-life lessons that were not explicitly addressed earlier: vision, human resources acumen, and magnanimity.

Vision. Most historians take some time to speculate as to Alexander's motives and aspirations, but I have eschewed such speculation. All great leaders I have met have a vision—some sort of a desirable image of the future, almost

1. W. W. Tarn, *Alexander the Great: Sources and Studies* (Cambridge: Oxford University Press, 1948), p. 145.

a dream. They also have a burning drive, a need, an obsession to see that vision come true. We do not and cannot know Alexander's vision. It may have been as small as revenge for his father's assassination. It may have been grander than what he achieved. We do know that he dithered in the eastern reaches of the empire with little effect. We know that his troops "mutinied" and stopped his furthest dreams. We also know, given his actions, that he was far ahead of his time, with regard, for example, to integrating cultures and his views on women, which I have not discussed in this book. He saw a future and a set of opportunities that no one around him seemed to share. Had he lived longer, we might be living in a more multiculturally harmonious world. The point is, while we do not know what it was, Alexander did have a vision. He had a drive to see that vision come to be. He was changing his world. To lead successfully, you need to have a vision and the drive to make it become real.

Human Resources Acumen. Alexander was a human resources genius. Look at the record. He knew the names of 10,000 soldiers. He ate and slept with his soldiers on the march. He ate sparingly and chose always to sleep cold. He led from the front and was frequently wounded with his soldiers. When the battle was over, he spent his time treating his soldiers' wounds because he was trained as a physician. He did this even when he had wounds of his own. Only when he had serious, debilitating wounds would he accept treatment before his soldiers. He later met with soldiers and encouraged them to discuss their heroic fights leading up to their wounds, almost certainly encouraging exaggeration. He generally discouraged rape and encouraged marriage. He paid dowries so his soldiers could marry local women. He forgave their debts. He shared the wealth seized from the empire with his soldiers, but they gladly burned it when it reduced the army's mobility. He poured out their proffered water in the desert and committed to sharing their fate. Such a set of actions reflects greatness. Alexander did not conquer the Persian Empire—his army did, under his leadership. For you to be a great leader, you need great followers, zealots really. The employees come first, because it is they who will make your dream come true.

Closely related to human resources acumen is the gift Alexander had of building relationships. Admittedly, part of his success was related to the times in which he lived. For example, he had multiple wives and he was bisexual, but these cultural aspects were expected among Greek noblemen. Certainly, such inclusiveness gave him a more accepting perspective on others' cultures. He forged adolescent relationships into lifelong partnerships. His Companions were his schoolmates with Aristotle. They conquered the world together. True, a few appeared to be disloyal and were killed, but they were the ultimate team. The rewards were great: Almost all inherited titles, kingdoms, wealth, and fame upon Alexander's death. Alexander befriended his foe's mother, and that friendship continued for life. He married "barbarians" against advisers' advice. His closest friend for life was the Companion and lover Hephaestion, who deserves his own biography. His relationship with his mother, given his mother's extreme religious beliefs (she claimed Alexander was conceived by a god), was remarkable. Much of his character was hers. In contrast to this extraordinary relationship, his relationship with his father was more variable, to say the least. Early, Alexander was the light of his father's life. At a very young age, he became a general in Philip's great army. Philip recognized how precocious his son was with the statement: "This kingdom is not big enough for the two of us, go find your own." However, later his father pulled a sword on him and banished him, declaring him no longer heir.

Magnanimity. Another theme that runs through Alexander the Great's life with high tension is that of magnanimity. The tension was because he was at times utterly ruthless, impossibly so, and then utterly magnanimous. One can parse the data and draw very different conclusions about his life: monster or saint. Obviously, both have some truth and both are wrong. The data to support the monster image comes from Thebes, the reduced hilltop town, Tyre, Cleitus, the Mallians, and all conspiracies. His saintly characteristics are more subtle: his relationship with his soldiers, his commitment to the Companions, Babylon, all ablutions and ceremonies throughout the campaign at local temples, his treatment of women (except the hilltop rapes and the Mallians), his wives and mistress, his friendship with Sisygambis (Darius's mother), his reverence for his own mother, and hundreds of other small actions. Despite the appearance to the contrary from the examples in Alexander's life, professionally (and perhaps naively) I counsel magnanimity in almost all situations. However, it is occasionally necessary or an absolute job requirement of a leader to crush, at the very least symbolically and visibly, certain people or causes. This is a tough lesson to teach, but a necessary one. Its application is part of the artistry of leadership.

Speaking now not from Alexander's experience but from my own, I offer two suggestions: Have heroes and read about them, and learn to tell stories.

To grow as a leader, you have to emulate someone. To learn on the job, from your mistakes especially, you need to have a context for the lesson. Heroes, such as Alexander, provide that context. It seems trite to encourage you to read history, but the reality is, that is where civilization stores its best heroes.

Finally, I am coming to understand that storytelling has a far greater role in leading than I had realized earlier in my career. This realization is not broadly shared yet, but I suspect it will permeate the leadership literature in decades to come. Storytelling is just a variant of great communication skills. It allows a leader to guide an organization toward the vision, toward the dream. Alexander repeatedly gave speeches that were laced with imagery closer to story than to fact. His skill at persuasion was remarkable, the mutiny in India notwithstanding. If you want to change the world, you better have a good story to tell.

APPENDIX: A BRIEF CHRONOLOGY OF ALEXANDER'S LIFE

B.C.	Major Events
359	Philip II is king of Macedonia.
356	Alexander is born, and later is educated by Aristotle.
336	Philip is assassinated; Alexander becomes king. Alexander consolidates Greece. Alexander conquers the Asia Minor coast.
334	Battle of Granicus.
333	Battle of Issus.
332	Siege of Tyre. Alexander enters and "liberates" Egypt.
331	Battle of Gaugamela.
330	Alexander conquers Mesopotamia. Destruction of Persepolis. Persian King Darius III murdered. Alexander initiates conquest of the Middle East.
327	Alexander invades India.

326 Battle at River Hydaspes.

324 Alexander returns to Susa and Babylon.

323 Alexander the Great dies.

BIBLIOGRAPHY

Ancient Sources

Arrian. *The Campaigns of Alexander.* Translated by Aubrey de Sélincourt. Harmondsworth, England: Penguin, 1958.

Curtius, Rufus. *The History of Alexander.* Harmondsworth, England: Penguin, 1984.

Diodorus, Siculus. *Alexander the Great.* Harmondsworth, England: Penguin, 1963.

Plutarch. *The Age of Alexander.* Harmondsworth, England: Penguin, 1973.

Scholarly Modern Sources

Adcock, F. E. *The Greek and Macedonian Art of War.* Berkeley, CA: University of California Press, 1957.

Bose, Partha. *Alexander the Great's Art of Strategy.* New York: Gotham, 2003.

Bosworth, A. B. *Conquest and Empire.* Cambridge: Cambridge University Press, 1988.

Dodge, Theodore Ayrault. *Alexander.* Boston: Houghton Mifflin, 1890.

Engels, Donald W. *Alexander the Great and the Logistics of the Macedonian Army.* Berkeley, CA: University of California Press, 1978.

Fildes, Alan, and Joann Fletcher. *Alexander the Great.* Los Angeles: Getty, 2001.

Fox, Robin Lane. *Alexander the Great.* London: Penguin, 1973.

Fuller, J. F. C. *The Generalship of Alexander the Great.* New Brunswick, NJ: Rutgers University Press, 1960.

Green, Peter. *Alexander of Macedon, 356–323* B.C. Berkeley, CA: University of California Press, 1991.

Grote, George. *A History of Greece,* Vol. X (reprint edition). New York: AMS Press, 1988.

Hammond, N. G. L. *The Genius of Alexander the Great.* Chapel Hill, NC: University of North Carolina Press, 1997.

Hanson, Victor Davis. *The Wars of the Ancient Greeks.* London: Cassell & Co, 1999.

Heckel, Waldemar. *The Wars of Alexander the Great, 336–323* B.C. Oxford: Osprey, 2002.

Marsden, E. W. *The Campaign of Gaugamela.* Liverpool: University Press, 1964.

O'Brien, John Maxwell. *Alexander the Great.* London: Routledge, 1992.

Rice, E. E. *Alexander the Great.* Phoenix Mill, England: Sutton Publishing, 1997.

Savill, Agnes. *Alexander the Great and His Time.* New York: Barnes & Noble, 1993.

Stoneman, Richard. *Alexander the Great.* London: Routledge, 1997.

Tarn, W. W. *Alexander the Great: Narrative.* Cambridge: Oxford University Press, 1951.

Tarn, W. W. *Alexander the Great: Sources and Studies.* Cambridge: Oxford University Press, 1948.

Tarn, W. W. *Hellenistic Military and Naval Developments.* Chicago: Ares Press, 1930.

Wilcken, Ulrich. *Alexander the Great.* New York: W. W. Norton, 1967.

"Popular" Modern Sources

Apostolou, Anna. *A Murder in Macedon.* New York: St. Martin's Press, 1997.

Lamb, Harold. *Alexander of Macedon.* New York: Bantam, 1946.

Renault, Mary. *Funeral Games.* New York: Pinnacle, 1981.

Renault, Mary. *The Nature of Alexander.* New York: Pantheon, 1975.

Renault, Mary. *The Persian Boy.* New York: Bantam, 1972.

Warry, John. *Alexander 334–323* B.C. Oxford: Osprey Publishing, 1991.

Warry, John. *Warfare in the Classical World.* Norman, OK: University of Oklahoma Press, 1995.

Wood, Michael. *In the Footsteps of Alexander the Great.* Berkeley, CA: University of California Press, 1997.

FURTHER READING

If you are seeking additional reading, allow me to presume to make some recommendations. Excepting the classics, which are rewarding but difficult reading, there are some wonderful options.

If you want a short, terrific historical chronology, you cannot do better than E. E. Rice's *Alexander the Great.* My favorite "scholarly" work (I put that word in quotes because Rice's work is very serious scholarship, though not as detailed as most historians may prefer) is A. B. Bosworth's *Conquest and Empire: The Reign of Alexander the Great.* A gorgeous, picture-rich history is the publication put out by the Getty Museum, Alan Fildes and Joann Fletcher's *Alexander the Great: Son of the Gods.* Probably the most succinct yet best "modern" history is W. W. Tarn's *Alexander the Great: Narrative,* although it is hard to find.

INDEX